LOUIS B. WRIGHT, General Editor. Director of the Folger Shakespeare Library from 1948 until his retirement in 1968, Dr. Wright has devoted over forty years to the study of the Shakespearean period. In 1926 he completed his doctoral thesis on "Vaudeville Elements in Elizabethan Drama" and subsequently published many articles on the stagecraft and theatre of Shakespeare's day. He is the author of *Middle-Class Culture in Elizabethan England* (1935), *Religion and Empire* (1942), *The Elizabethans' America* (1965), and many other books and essays on the history and literature of the Tudor and Stuart periods, including *Shakespeare for Everyman* (1964). Dr. Wright has taught at the universities of North Carolina, California at Los Angeles, Michigan, Minnesota, and other American institutions. From 1932 to 1948 he was instrumental in developing the research program of the Henry E. Huntington Library and Art Gallery. During his tenure as Director, the Folger Shakespeare Library became one of the leading research institutions of the world for the study of the backgrounds of Anglo-American civilization.

VIRGINIA A. LaMAR, Assistant Editor. A member of the staff of the Folger Shakespeare Library from 1946 until her death in 1968, Miss LaMar served as research assistant to the Director and as Executive Secretary. Prior to 1946 Miss LaMar had been a secretary in the British Admiralty Delegation in Washington, D.C., receiving the King's Medal in 1945 for her services. She was coeditor of the *Historie of Travell into Virginia Britania* by William Strachey, published by The Hakluyt Society in 1953, and author of *English Dress in the Age of Shakespeare* and *Travel and Roads in England* in the "Folger Booklets on Tudor and Stuart Civilization" series.

The Folger Shakespeare Library

THE TEMPEST

By

WILLIAM

SHAKESPEARE

WASHINGTON SQUARE PRESS

THE TEMPEST

A *Washington Square Press* edition

1st printing.........................June, 1961
9th printing.........................May, 1970

A new edition of a distinguished literary work now made available in an inexpensive, well-designed format

L

Published by Washington Square Press,
a division of Simon & Schuster, Inc., 630 Fifth Avenue, New York, N.Y.

WASHINGTON SQUARE PRESS editions are distributed in the U.S. by Simon & Schuster, Inc., 630 Fifth Avenue, New York, N.Y. 10020 and in Canada by Simon & Schuster of Canada, Ltd., Richmond Hill, Ontario, Canada.

Preface

This edition of *The Tempest* is designed to make available a readable text of one of Shakespeare's most popular plays. In the centuries since Shakespeare many changes have occurred in the meanings of words, and some clarification of Shakespeare's vocabulary may be helpful. To provide the reader with necessary notes in the most accessible format, we have placed them on the pages facing the text that they explain. We have tried to make these notes as brief and simple as possible. Preliminary to the text we have also included a brief statement of essential information about Shakespeare and his stage. Readers desiring more detailed information should refer to the books suggested in the references, and if still further information is needed, the bibliographies in those books will provide the necessary clues to the literature of the subject.

The early texts of all of Shakespeare's plays provide only inadequate stage directions, and it is conventional for modern editors to add many that clarify the action. Such additions, and additions to entrances, are placed in square brackets.

All illustrations are from material in the Folger Library collections.

L. B. W.
V. A. L.

December, 1960

Island of Magic

The Tempest was the last entire play that Shakespeare wrote before he left London to lead the life of a man of property in Stratford. During the score of years that he had been active in London, he had seen many changes in the theatre and in popular taste. Shrewdly sensitive to what the public wanted, Shakespeare had always managed not only to provide plays that suited the fashion but also to write in a manner that transcended the mood of the moment. Few Elizabethan playwrights were more conscious of the box office than Shakespeare, but, like George Bernard Shaw in a later time, he had the genius to put together dramas with an enduring quality. In London Shakespeare had prospered. He had invested his money wisely, bought the best house in Stratford, and, as he sat down to write *The Tempest*, was looking forward to taking his ease in his garden at New Place where he might contemplate his London successes and write a bit when it suited him. Life could be calm and serene.

The King's Men in 1611 needed a play for court performance that would appeal to King James and his nobles and later serve for the London public. The master craftsman of the company, William Shakespeare, was the man to write such a play, even if he had his mind on retirement and was probably anxious to get away from the hurly-burly of London. So Shakespeare complied and provided the King's Men with a play performed at court on November 1, 1611, and again in the winter of 1612–1613, probably as part of the wedding festivities of King James's daughter Elizabeth to Frederick, the Elector Palatine and briefly the King of Bohemia. It was a play that pleased the dramatist's contemporaries and has pleased audiences from that day to this, a mature play with a serene outlook, with just the right mixture of fantasy, philosophy, spectacle, and humor to delight King James and many who have come after him. The days of the great cosmic tragedies, the stirring history plays, and the more boisterous comedies were now behind Shakespeare. A new style of drama had gained popularity on the London stages, the tragicomedies and romances of Francis Beaumont and John Fletcher, collaborators who now had a great following and were setting the pace for other dramatists. If Shakespeare's later plays, *Winter's Tale, Cymbeline,* and *The Tempest* are not precisely imitative of the younger playwrights, they nevertheless reflect the fashion that Beaumont and Fletcher exemplified. Shakespeare was too original and experienced a dramatist to need to imitate lesser writers and he could conform to the new style and still outshine them all. *The Tempest* is proof of this skill.

Like many of the plays of Beaumont and Fletcher, *The Tempest* is set in a timeless opera-land. To be sure, we are concerned with a Duke of Milan and a King of Naples, but they are two characters unknown to history and their Naples and Milan are mere names, not clearly designated localities. The action takes place on an island even more vague in its geographical setting. It must lie somewhere in the Mediterranean, for we are told that the shipwrecked party had encountered a storm on the return voyage from Tunis where the King of Naples' daughter had married a totally unhistorical king of that place. Shakespeare is dealing with realms of fancy, not reality.

The sources of the play are also somewhat vague and dispersed, a fact that has worried scholars who like to find a definite and provable genesis for each play. It is possible that some previous play had employed Shakespeare's precise theme, but if so, no one has found it. It is possible that some forgotten Italian story known to him had this plot, but if so, it is lost to us. Plot elements in *The Tempest* are common to romance and folklore and appear in many places. A German play, *Die Schöne Sidea*, by Jacob Ayrer of Nuremberg, dating from sometime before 1605, has a magician whose daughter falls in love with his enemy's son; some of the situations are also similar to those in *The Tempest*, but there is no evidence that Shakespeare ever saw the German play. Perhaps Ayrer and Shakespeare drew their inspirations from some common source. Four Italian *scenari* for *commedia dell' arte* performances, published by Ferdinando Neri in 1913 from a Renaissance manuscript, contain scenes that vaguely resemble comic situations in *The Tempest*. Since the *commedia dell' arte* was known in Shakespeare's London, it is argued that he may have seen one of these *scenari*, but the parallels are not close enough to be convincing. Shakespeare, like any creative artist, drew upon his memory for many elements that went into this play of the imagination.

Many years ago, Rudyard Kipling, himself interested in the intellectual process of the creative writer, turned his own imagination to the problem of the inspiration of *The Tempest*. In a letter published in the London *Spectator* for July 2, 1898, Kipling mentioned the contemporary excitement over the wreck of Sir George

Somers and Sir Thomas Gates in the *Sea Adventure*
on Bermuda in 1609, and proceeded to give his notion
of how the dramatist came to pick up the incidents
that he wove into his play, perhaps from "nothing
more promising in fact than the chattering of a half-
tipsy sailor at the theatre." He imagines Shakespeare
overhearing a sailor talking about a grievous storm, of
being driven aground on a bewitched island, of a
sailor who salvaged a butt of sack, and of many things
that a lively imagination could re-create into a play.
Kipling's letter is a useful lesson in the way that a
writer may organize scattered suggestions into an or-
ganic unity. It is also an antidote to the academic
notion that the creative writer invariably draws out
of the library a batch of books and laboriously patches
together his play from these sources.

Shakespeare's imagination, we know, was stimulated
by stories of the wreck of the Gates and Somers ex-
pedition on Bermuda, and he used ideas and suggestions from some of the accounts of the wreck of the
Sea Adventure. Silvester Jourdain's *A Discovery of the
Barmudas* (1610) gave an eyewitness account of the
wreck and was much talked about on its publication.
The Virginia Company published an official report of
the event as *A True Declaration of the Estate of the
Colonie in Virginia* (1610), and Richard Rich wrote
a ballad on the subject, *Newes from Virginia* (1610).
But the account that seems to have colored Shakespeare's thinking more than any other was William
Strachey's *A True Reportory of the Wracke and Re-
demption of Sir Thomas Gates, Knight,* which, so far
as we know, first appeared in print in 1625 in Samuel
Purchas' *Hakluytus Posthumus, or Purchas His Pil-
grimes.* But Strachey, who had gone out as secretary
of the Virginia Company, was closely associated with

the theatrical group of which Shakespeare was a member, and his *True Reportory*, sent back to England soon after the wreck, undoubtedly was read by Shakespeare in manuscript. The colonization of Virginia had stirred the imagination of many writers besides Shakespeare. The Earl of Southampton, Shakespeare's patron, was an investor in the Virginia Company and was deeply concerned with the ventures overseas. With all of the talk and writing about the New World, and in 1610, just as Shakespeare was gathering material for his new play, with the excitement over the episode of Sir Thomas Gates and Sir George Somers on Bermuda, it would have been strange if some of this had not found a reflection in *The Tempest*.

Other reading by the dramatist is reflected in the play, especially travel accounts, which were exceedingly popular. In Richard Eden's *History of Travayle* (1577) he may have found the name of a Patagonian god, Setebos. And from Florio's translation of Montaigne, in the essay "Of the Caniballes," he borrowed material for Gonzalo's description of an idealized Golden Age in Act II, Sc. i. *The Tempest* contains Shakespeare's commentary on the New World, but patriotic Americans have perhaps read more into the play than the words warrant.

Whether Shakespeare intended *The Tempest* to be an allegory full of deep significance is doubtful, though many allegorical interpretations of the play have been attempted. With much common sense, Sir Edmund Chambers has written: "I have rejected the temptation to suggest that just as Ariel symbolizes the spirit of poetry brought by Shakespeare into the service of the creative imagination, so Caliban signifies the spirit of prose, born of Sycorax who is controversial theology, and imperfectly subdued by Shakespeare to the same purpose. There are some who follow Renan in taking Caliban for a type of Demos, and regard his desire to 'nor scrape trenchering nor wash dish' as eminently characteristic of political ideals which aim at nothing higher than the escape from reasonable labor. Of any political intention on Shakespeare's part in *The Tempest* I am profoundly skeptical."

Caliban has even been interpreted as Shakespeare's prophetic anticipation of Darwin's missing link, and sundry other interpretations have been found in Shakespeare's contrast between the earthy, half-human creature and the ethereal Ariel. Whatever allegorical interpretation may be given Caliban, he was interpreted by contemporary audiences as a stage representation of one of the monstrous creatures described by travelers and explorers from Mandeville to Raleigh. Some of these had eyes in their chests instead of their heads, while others were accustomed to stand on one foot and hold the other over their heads like an umbrella. Elizabethans had heard many strange tales of the world beyond the seas and were prepared to accept as veritable any monster or marvel.

Many critics, including Sir Edmund Chambers, have seen in the episode of Prospero's breaking of his staff and burying his book, Shakespeare's renunciation of his active life in London and his return to his "dukedom of Milan" in Stratford. "May one venture to think," Sir Edmund asks, "that something better and more spiritual than this merely respectable instinct helped to account for his flight? Is it possible that, in 1611, Shakespeare heard Warwickshire calling with a voice that would not be denied? London was a growing city in the early seventeenth century, and a note of revolt from urban life, hardly heard since the days of the poets of imperial Rome, was beginning to steal into literature." Certainly, the life of an actor and dramatist was not one to be envied. Actors still occupied no position of respectability and they had hardly emerged from the lowly status beside rogues and sturdy beggars which they had occupied during the previous reign. Theatrical writing in 1611 still was hardly considered literature. For a man who could afford to say good-by to the hard life of the theatre, there was little temptation to remain, even though Shakespeare himself must have been conscious that his plays possessed a charm that made him a magician among writers. There is good reason to believe that he was glad to give up that magic for a better life in a pleasant town in Warwickshire.

The Tempest, unlike most of Shakespeare's plays, carefully observes the unities of time and place. Structurally the play has some of the characteristics of the type of entertainment that Ben Jonson and Inigo Jones, the architect, were making popular at court. This was the masque, a pageant-like performance of dance, music, dialogue, and spectacle, frequently with scenes from mythology. The typical masque has dainty and graceful music and dance numbers, followed by an antimasque of grotesque characters who serve as foils and as contrast. In *The Tempest* we have Ariel and the courtly figures in contrast with Caliban and the drunken sailors, Stephano and Trinculo, who provide comic effects. In Act IV Prospero by his magic calls up a formal mythological pageant that is characteristic of the court masque. Indeed, some critics have argued that Act IV was a later insertion by another hand, but there is no evidence to indicate that Shakespeare did not compose it as part of his own masquelike play. Act IV provides precisely the kind of spectacle that was fashionable and that the court expected.

STAGE HISTORY

The popularity of *The Tempest* has persisted from its first performance to the present time, though few plays of Shakespeare have offered greater temptations for alteration and adaptation to "improve" the spectacle.

After the Restoration, an adaptation of *The Tempest* by Sir William Davenant and John Dryden was performed in 1667 at Lincoln's Inn Fields. Among their "improvements" was the addition of a man who had never seen a woman, a sister for Miranda, a sister for Caliban, and a love for Ariel, with comic additions to the sailor scenes. This hodgepodge was so popular that Thomas Shadwell in 1674 further revised it into an opera with music by Henry Purcell. This version, dependent upon scenery and music, was long popular and was seen in the theatre until late in the eighteenth century. David Garrick, the actor-manager of Drury Lane, wrote a libretto for a new operatic version with music by John Christopher Smith, which was produced in 1756.

Frederick Reynolds was responsible for a third operatic version produced in London in 1821. The two older operas based on *The Tempest* had continued to flourish but were finally vanquished by Reynolds' musical version and an effective production of the original play by William Charles Macready in 1838.

The Tempest appeared at intervals during the nineteenth and early twentieth centuries on both sides of the Atlantic, but producers in nearly every instance depended upon spectacular staging for their effects. Shakespeare himself in planning the original court performances had designed his play for spectacle, so that purists, however much they may object to the taste and judgment displayed by producers of spectacles, cannot complain too validly about violations of the intent of the dramatist. We do not know what the version produced at the wedding festivities of Princess Elizabeth in 1613 may have looked like. The purest versions of *The Tempest* performed during the first half of this century were productions by amateurs who did not have the material facilities for extravaganzas. A television production of *The Tempest* in 1960 introduced many tricks of illusion, with a minuscule Ariel flitting about the air, and a very fishy Caliban creeping about the ground, but the net effect was less than satisfactory. Although *The Tempest* is a difficult play to produce and interpret on the stage, it has remained popular with both spectators and readers.

PUBLICATION

The first printing of *The Tempest* occurred in the First Folio of 1623, where the play was given the place of honor at the beginning of the volume. It was more carefully edited than most of the other plays and has more elaborate stage directions than is customary. The care with which the copy for the First Folio was prepared has led some editors to believe that a transcript was made for Heminges and Condell to use as printer's copy. The present text is based on the First Folio version with a minimum of emendations.

THE AUTHOR

As early as 1598 Shakespeare was so well known as a literary and dramatic craftsman that Francis Meres, in his *Palladis Tamia: Wits Treasury*, referred in flattering terms to him as "mellifluous and honey-tongued Shakespeare," famous for his *Venus and Adonis*, his *Lucrece*, and "his sugared sonnets," which were circulating "among his private friends." Meres observes further that "as Plautus and Seneca are accounted the best for comedy and tragedy among the Latins, so Shakespeare among the English is the most excellent in both kinds for the stage," and he mentions a dozen plays that had made a name for Shakespeare. He concludes with the remark "that the Muses would speak with Shakespeare's fine filed phrase if they would speak English."

To those acquainted with the history of the Elizabethan and Jacobean periods, it is incredible that anyone should be so naïve or ignorant as to doubt the reality of Shakespeare as the author of the plays that bear his name. Yet so much nonsense has been written about other "candidates" for the plays that it is well to remind readers that no credible evidence that would stand up in a court of law has ever been adduced to prove either that Shakespeare did not write his plays or that anyone else wrote them. All the theories offered for the authorship of Francis Bacon, the Earl of Derby, the Earl of Oxford, the Earl of Hertford, Christopher Marlowe, and a score of other candidates are mere conjectures spun from the active imaginations of persons who confuse hypothesis and conjecture with evidence.

As Meres' statement of 1598 indicates, Shakespeare was already a popular playwright whose name carried weight at the box office. The obvious reputation of Shakespeare as early as 1598 makes the effort to prove him a myth one of the most absurd in the history of human perversity.

The anti-Shakespeareans talk darkly about a plot of

vested interests to maintain the authorship of Shakespeare. Nobody has any vested interest in Shakespeare, but every scholar is interested in the truth and in the quality of evidence advanced by special pleaders who set forth hypotheses in place of facts.

The anti-Shakespeareans base their arguments upon a few simple premises, all of them false. These false premises are that Shakespeare was an unlettered yokel without any schooling, that nothing is known about Shakespeare, and that only a noble lord or the equivalent in background could have written the plays. The facts are that more is known about Shakespeare than about most dramatists of his day, that he had a very good education, acquired in the Stratford Grammar School, that the plays show no evidence of profound book learning, and that the knowledge of kings and courts evident in the plays is no greater than any intelligent young man could have picked up at second hand. Most anti-Shakespeareans are naïve and betray an obvious snobbery. The author of their favorite plays, they imply, must have had a college diploma framed and hung on his study wall like the one in their dentist's office, and obviously so great a writer must have had a title or some equally significant evidence of exalted social background. They forget that genius has a way of cropping up in unexpected places and that none of the great creative writers of the world got his inspiration in a college or university course.

William Shakespeare was the son of John Shakespeare of Stratford-upon-Avon, a substantial citizen of that small but busy market town in the center of the rich agricultural county of Warwick. John Shakespeare kept a shop, what we would call a general store; he dealt in wool and other produce and gradually acquired property. As a youth, John Shakespeare had learned the trade of glover and leather worker. There is no contemporary evidence that the elder Shakespeare was a butcher, though the anti-Shakespeareans like to talk about the ignorant "butcher's boy of Stratford." Their only evidence is a statement by gossipy John Aubrey, more than a century after William Shakespeare's birth, that young William followed his father's trade, and when he killed a calf, "he would do it in a high style and make a speech." We would like to believe the story true, but Aubrey is not a very credible witness.

John Shakespeare probably continued to operate a farm at Snitterfield that his father had leased. He married Mary Arden, daughter of his father's landlord, a man of some property. The third of their eight children was William, baptized on April 26, 1564, and probably born three days before. At least, it is conventional to celebrate April 23 as his birthday.

The Stratford records give considerable information about John Shakespeare. We know that he held several municipal offices including those of alderman and mayor. In 1580 he was in some sort of legal difficulty and was fined for neglecting a summons of the Court of Queen's Bench requiring him to appear at Westminster and be bound over to keep the peace.

As a citizen and alderman of Stratford, John Shakespeare was entitled to send his son to the grammar school free. Though the records are lost, there can be no reason to doubt that this is where young William received his education. As any student of the period knows, the grammar schools provided the basic education in Latin learning and literature. The Elizabethan grammar school is not to be confused with modern grammar schools. Many cultivated men of the day received all their formal education in the grammar schools. At the universities in this period a student would have received little training that would have inspired him to be a creative writer. At Stratford young Shakespeare would have acquired a familiarity with Latin and some little knowledge of Greek. He would have read Latin authors and become acquainted with the plays of Plautus and Terence. Undoubtedly, in this period of his life he received that stimulation to read and explore for himself the world of ancient and modern history which he later utilized in his plays. The youngster who does not acquire this type of intellectual curiosity *before* college days rarely develops as a result of a college course the kind of mind Shakespeare demonstrated. His learning in books was anything but profound, but he clearly had the probing curiosity that sent him in search of information, and he had a keenness in the observation of nature and of humankind that finds reflection in his poetry.

There is little documentation for Shakespeare's boyhood. There is little reason why there should be. Nobody knew that he was going to be a dramatist about whom any scrap of information would be prized in the centuries to come. He was merely an active and vigorous youth of Stratford, perhaps assisting his father in his business, and no Boswell bothered to write down facts about him. The most important record that we have is a marriage license issued by the Bishop of Worcester on November 28, 1582, to permit William Shakespeare to marry Anne Hathaway, seven or eight years his senior; furthermore, the Bishop permitted the marriage after reading the banns only once instead of three times, evidence of the desire for haste. The need was explained on May 26, 1583, when the christening of Susanna, daughter of William and Anne Shakespeare, was recorded at Stratford. Two years later, on

February 2, 1585, the records show the birth of twins to the Shakespeares, a boy and a girl who were christened Hamnet and Judith.

What William Shakespeare was doing in Stratford during the early years of his married life, or when he went to London, we do not know. It has been conjectured that he tried his hand at schoolteaching, but that is a mere guess. There is a legend that he left Stratford to escape a charge of poaching in the park of Sir Thomas Lucy of Charlecote, but there is no proof of this. There is also a legend that when first he came to London, he earned his living by holding horses outside a playhouse and presently was given employment inside, but there is nothing better than eighteenth-century hearsay for this. How Shakespeare broke into the London theatres as a dramatist and actor we do not know. But lack of information is not surprising, for Elizabethans did not write their autobiographies, and we know even less about the lives of many writers and some men of affairs than we know about Shakespeare. By 1592 he was so well established and popular that he incurred the envy of the dramatist and pamphleteer Robert Greene, who referred to him as an "upstart crow . . . in his own conceit the only Shake-scene in a country." From this time onward, contemporary allusions and references in legal documents enable the scholar to chart Shakespeare's career with greater accuracy than is possible with most other Elizabethan dramatists.

By 1594 Shakespeare was a member of the company of actors known as the Lord Chamberlain's Men. After the accession of James I, in 1603, the company would have the sovereign for their patron and would be known as the King's Men. During the period of its greatest prosperity, this company would have as its

principal theatres the Globe and the Blackfriars. Shakespeare was both an actor and a shareholder in the company. Tradition has assigned him such acting roles as
Adam in *As You Like It* and the Ghost in *Hamlet,* a
modest place on the stage that suggests that he may
have had other duties in the management of the company. Such conclusions, however, are based on surmise.

What we do know is that his plays were popular and
that he was highly successful in his vocation. His first
play may have been *The Comedy of Errors,* acted perhaps in 1591. Certainly this was one of his earliest
plays. The three parts of *Henry VI* were acted sometime between 1590 and 1592. Critics are not in agreement about precisely how much Shakespeare wrote of
these three plays. *Richard III* probably dates from
1593. With this play Shakespeare captured the imagination of Elizabethan audiences, then enormously interested in historical plays. With *Richard III* Shakespeare also gave an interpretation pleasing to the Tudors of the rise to power of the grandfather of Queen
Elizabeth. From this time onward, Shakespeare's plays
followed on the stage in rapid succession: *Titus An-
dronicus, The Taming of the Shrew, The Two Gentlemen of Verona, Love's Labour's Lost, Romeo and
Juliet, Richard II, A Midsummer Night's Dream, King
John, The Merchant of Venice, Henry IV (Parts 1 and
2), Much Ado About Nothing, Henry V, Julius Cæsar,
As You Like It, Twelfth Night, Hamlet, The Merry
Wives of Windsor, All's Well That Ends Well, Measure for Measure, Othello, King Lear,* and nine others
that followed before Shakespeare retired completely,
about 1613.

In the course of his career in London, he made
enough money to enable him to retire to Stratford with
a competence. His purchase on May 4, 1597, of New

Place, then the second-largest dwelling in Stratford, a "pretty house of brick and timber," with a handsome garden, indicates his increasing prosperity. There his wife and children lived while he busied himself in the London theatres. The summer before he acquired New Place, his life was darkened by the death of his only son, Hamnet, a child of eleven. In May, 1602, Shakespeare purchased one hundred and seven acres of fertile farmland near Stratford and a few months later bought a cottage and garden across the alley from New Place. About 1611, he seems to have returned permanently to Stratford, for the next year a legal document refers to him as "William Shakespeare of Stratford-upon-Avon . . . gentleman." To achieve the desired appellation of gentleman, William Shakespeare had seen to it that the College of Heralds in 1596 granted his father a coat of arms. In one step he thus became a second-generation gentleman.

Shakespeare's daughter Susanna made a good match in 1607 with Dr. John Hall, a prominent and prosperous Stratford physician. His second daughter, Judith, did not marry until she was thirty-two years old, and then, under somewhat scandalous circumstances, she married Thomas Quiney, a Stratford vintner. On March 25, 1616, Shakespeare made his will, bequeathing his landed property to Susanna, £300 to Judith, certain sums to other relatives, and his second-best bed to his wife, Anne. Much has been made of the second-best bed, but the legacy probably indicates only that Anne liked that particular bed. Shakespeare, following the practice of the time, may have already arranged with Susanna for his wife's care. Finally, on April 23, 1616, the anniversary of his birth, William Shakespeare died, and he was buried on April 25 within the chancel of Trinity Church, as befitted an honored citizen. On

August 6, 1623, a few months before the publication of the collected edition of Shakespeare's plays, Anne Shakespeare joined her husband in death.

THE PUBLICATION OF HIS PLAYS

During his lifetime Shakespeare made no effort to publish any of his plays, though eighteen appeared in print in single-play editions known as quartos. Some of these are corrupt versions known as "bad quartos." No quarto, so far as is known, had the author's approval. Plays were not considered "literature" any more than most radio and television scripts today are considered literature. Dramatists sold their plays outright to the theatrical companies and it was usually considered in the company's interest to keep plays from getting into print. To achieve a reputation as a man of letters, Shakespeare wrote his *Sonnets* and his narrative poems, *Venus and Adonis* and *The Rape of Lucrece,* but he probably never dreamed that his plays would establish his reputation as a literary genius. Only Ben Jonson, a man known for his colossal conceit, had the crust to call his plays *Works,* as he did when he published an edition in 1616. But men laughed at Ben Jonson.

After Shakespeare's death, two of his old colleagues in the King's Men, John Heminges and Henry Condell, decided that it would be a good thing to print, in more accurate versions than were then available, the plays already published and eighteen additional plays not previously published in quarto. In 1623 appeared *Mr. William Shakespeares Comedies, Histories, & Tragedies. Published according to the True Originall Copies. London. Printed by Isaac Iaggard and Ed. Blount.* This was the famous First Folio, a work that had the authority of Shakespeare's associates. The only play commonly attributed to Shakespeare that was omitted in the First Folio was *Pericles*. In their preface, "To the great Variety of Readers," Heminges and Condell state that whereas "you were abused with diverse stolen and surreptitious copies, maimed and deformed by the frauds and stealths of injurious impostors that exposed them, even those are now offered to your view cured and perfect of their limbs; and all the rest, absolute in their numbers, as he conceived them." What they used for printer's copy is one of the vexed problems of scholarship, and skilled bibliographers have devoted years of study to the question of the relation of the "copy" for the First Folio to Shakespeare's manuscripts. In some cases it is clear that the editors corrected printed quarto versions of the plays, probably by comparison with playhouse scripts. Whether these scri ts were in Shakespeare's autograph is anybody's guess. No manuscript of any play in Shakespeare's handwriting has survived. Indeed, very few play manuscripts from this period by any author are extant. The Tudor and Stuart periods had not yet learned to prize autographs and authors' original manuscripts.

Since the First Folio contains eighteen plays not previously printed, it is the only source for these. For the other eighteen, which had appeared in quarto versions, the First Folio also has the authority of an edition prepared and overseen by Shakespeare's colleagues and professional associates. But since editorial standards in 1623 were far from strict, and Heminges and Condell were actors rather than editors by profession, the texts are sometimes careless. The printing and proofreading of the First Folio also left much to be desired, and some garbled passages have to be corrected and emended. The "good quarto" texts have to be taken into account in preparing a modern edition.

Because of the great popularity of Shakespeare through the centuries, the First Folio has become a prized book, but it is not a very rare one, for it is estimated that 238 copies are extant. The Folger Shakespeare Library in Washington, D.C., has seventy-nine copies of the First Folio, collected by the founder, Henry Clay Folger, who believed that a collation of as many texts as possible would reveal significant facts about the text of Shakespeare's plays. Dr. Charlton Hinman, using an ingenious machine of his own invention for mechanical collating, has made discoveries that throw light on Shakespeare's text and on printing practices of the day.

The probability is that the First Folio of 1623 had an edition of between 1,000 and 1,250 copies. It is believed that it sold for £1, which made it an expensive book, for £1 in 1623 was equivalent to something between $40 and $50 in modern purchasing power.

During the seventeenth century, Shakespeare was sufficiently popular to warrant three later editions in folio size, the Second Folio of 1632, the Third Folio of 1663–1664, and the Fourth Folio of 1685. The Third Folio added six other plays ascribed to Shakespeare, but these are apocryphal.

THE SHAKESPEAREAN THEATRE

The theatres in which Shakespeare's plays were performed were vastly different from those we know today. The stage was a platform that jutted out into the area now occupied by the first two rows of seats on the main floor, what is called the "orchestra" in America and the "pit" in England. This platform had no curtain to come down at the ends of acts and scenes. And although simple stage properties were available, the Elizabethan theatre lacked both the machinery and the elaborate movable scenery of the modern theatre. In the rear of the platform stage was a curtained area that could be used as an inner room, a tomb, or any such scene that might be required. A balcony above this inner room, and perhaps balconies on the sides of the stage, could represent the upper deck of a ship, the entry to Juliet's room, or a prison window. A trap door in the stage provided an entrance for ghosts and devils from the nether regions, and a similar trap in the canopied structure over the stage, known as the "heavens," made it possible to let down angels on a rope. These primitive stage arrangements help to account for many elements in Elizabethan plays. For example, since there was no curtain, the dramatist frequently felt the necessity of writing into his play action to clear the stage at the ends of acts and scenes. The funeral march at the end of *Hamlet* is not there merely for atmosphere; Shakespeare had to get the corpses off the stage. The lack of scenery also freed the dramatist from undue concern about the exact location of his sets, and the physical relation of his various settings to each other did not have to be worked out with the same precision as in the modern theatre.

Before London had buildings designed exclusively for theatrical entertainment, plays were given in inns and taverns. The characteristic inn of the period had an inner courtyard with rooms opening onto balconies overlooking the yard. Players could set up their temporary stages at one end of the yard and audiences could find seats on the balconies out of the weather. The poorer sort could stand or sit on the cobblestones in the yard, which was open to the sky. The first theatres followed this construction, and throughout the Elizabethan period the large public theatres had a yard in front of the stage open to the weather, with two or three tiers of covered balconies extending around the theatre. This physical structure again influenced the writing of plays. Because a dramatist wanted the actors to be heard, he frequently wrote into his play orations that could be delivered with declamatory effect. He also provided spectacle, buffoonery, and broad jests to keep the riotous groundlings in the yard entertained and quiet.

In another respect the Elizabethan theatre differed greatly from ours. It had no actresses. All women's roles were taken by boys, sometimes recruited from the boys' choirs of the London churches. Some of these youths acted their roles with great skill and the Elizabethans did not seem to be aware of any incongruity. The first actresses on the professional English stage appeared after the Restoration of Charles II, in 1660, when exiled Englishmen brought back from France practices of the French stage.

London in the Elizabethan period, as now, was the center of theatrical interest, though wandering actors from time to time traveled through the country performing in inns, halls, and the houses of the nobility. The first professional playhouse, called simply The Theatre, was erected by James Burbage, father of Shakespeare's colleague Richard Burbage, in 1576 on lands of the old Holywell Priory adjacent to Finsbury Fields, a playground and park area just north of the city walls. It had the advantage of being outside the city's jurisdiction and yet was near enough to be easily accessible. Soon after The Theatre was opened, another playhouse called The Curtain was erected in the same neighborhood. Both of these playhouses had open courtyards and were probably polygonal in shape.

About the time The Curtain opened, Richard Farrant, Master of the Children of the Chapel Royal at

Windsor and of St. Paul's, conceived the idea of opening a "private" theatre in the old monastery buildings of the Blackfriars, not far from St. Paul's Cathedral in the heart of the city. This theatre was ostensibly to train the choirboys in plays for presentation at Court, but Farrant managed to present plays to paying audiences and achieved considerable success until aristocratic neighbors complained and had the theatre closed. This first Blackfriars Theatre was significant, however, because it popularized the boy actors in a professional way and it paved the way for a second theatre in the Blackfriars, which Shakespeare's company took over more than thirty years later. By the last years of the sixteenth century, London had at least six professional theatres and still others were erected during the reign of James I.

The Globe Theatre, the playhouse that most people connect with Shakespeare, was erected early in 1599 on the Bankside, the area across the Thames from the city. Its construction had a dramatic beginning, for on the night of December 28, 1598, James Burbage's sons, Cuthbert and Richard, gathered together a crew who tore down the old theatre in Holywell and carted the timbers across the river to a site that they had chosen for a new playhouse. The reason for this clandestine operation was a row with the landowner over the lease of the Holywell property. The site chosen for the Globe was another playground outside of the city's jurisdiction, a region of somewhat unsavory character. Not far away was the Bear Garden, an amphitheatre devoted to the baiting of bears and bulls. This was also the region occupied by many houses of ill fame licensed by the Bishop of Winchester and the source of substantial revenue to him. But it was easily accessible either from London Bridge or by means of the cheap boats operated by the London watermen, and it had the great advantage of being beyond the authority of the Puritanical aldermen of London, who frowned on plays because they lured apprentices from work, filled their heads with improper ideas, and generally exerted a bad influence. The aldermen also complained that the crowds drawn together in the theatre helped to spread the plague.

The Globe was the handsomest theatre up to its time. It was a large building, apparently octagonal in shape and open like its predecessors to the sky in the center, but capable of seating a large audience in its covered balconies. To erect and operate the Globe, the Burbages organized a syndicate composed of the leading members of the dramatic company, of which Shakespeare was a member. Since it was open to the weather and depended on natural light, plays had to be given in the afternoon. This caused no hardship in the long afternoons of an English summer, but in the winter the weather was a great handicap and discouraged all except the hardiest. For that reason, in 1608 Shakespeare's company was glad to take over the lease of the second Blackfriars Theatre, a substantial, roomy hall reconstructed within the framework of the old monastery building. This theatre was protected from the weather and its stage was artificially lighted by chandeliers of candles. This became the winter playhouse for Shakespeare's company and at once proved so popular that the congestion of traffic created an embarrassing problem. Stringent regulations had to be made for the movement of coaches in the vicinity. Shakespeare's company continued to use the Globe during the summer months. In 1613 a squib fired from a cannon during a performance of *Henry VIII* fell on the thatched roof and the Globe burned to the ground. The next year it was rebuilt.

London had other famous theatres. The Rose, just west of the Globe, was built by Philip Henslowe, a semiliterate denizen of the Bankside, who became one of the most important theatrical owners and producers of the Tudor and Stuart periods. What is more important for historians, he kept a detailed account book, which provides much of our information about theatrical history in his time. Another famous theatre on the Bankside was the Swan, which a Dutch priest, Johannes de Witt, visited in 1596. The crude drawing of the stage which he made was copied by his friend Arend van Buchell; it is one of the important pieces of contemporary evidence for theatrical construction. Among the other theatres, the Fortune, north of the city, on Golding Lane, and the Red Bull, even farther away from the city, off St. John's Street, were the most popular. The Red Bull, much frequented by apprentices, favored sensational and sometimes rowdy plays.

The actors who kept all of these theatres going were organized into companies under the protection of some noble patron. Traditionally actors had enjoyed a low reputation. In some of the ordinances they were classed as vagrants; in the phraseology of the time, "rogues, vagabonds, sturdy beggars, and common players" were all listed together as undesirables. To escape penalties often meted out to these characters, organized groups of actors managed to gain the protection of various personages of high degree. In the later years of Elizabeth's reign, a group flourished under the name of the Queen's Men; another group had the protection of the Lord Admiral and were known as the Lord Admiral's Men. Edward Alleyn, son-in-law of Philip Henslowe, was the leading spirit in the Lord Admiral's Men. Besides the adult companies, troupes of boy actors from time to time also enjoyed considerable popularity. Among these were the Children of Paul's and the Children of the Chapel Royal.

The company with which Shakespeare had a long association had for its first patron Henry Carey, Lord Hunsdon, the Lord Chamberlain, and hence they were known as the Lord Chamberlain's Men. After the accession of James I, they became the King's Men. This company was the great rival of the Lord Admiral's Men, managed by Henslowe and Alleyn.

All was not easy for the players in Shakespeare's time, for the aldermen of London were always eager for an excuse to close up the Blackfriars and any other theatres in their jurisdiction. The theatres outside the jurisdiction of London were not immune from interference, for they might be shut up by order of the Privy Council for meddling in politics or for various other offenses, or they might be closed in time of plague lest they spread infection. During plague times, the actors usually went on tour and played the provinces wherever they could find an audience. Particularly frightening were the plagues of 1592–1594 and 1613 when the theatres closed and the players, like many other Londoners, had to take to the country.

Though players had a low social status, they enjoyed great popularity, and one of the favorite forms of entertainment at court was the performance of plays. To be commanded to perform at court conferred great prestige upon a company of players, and printers frequently noted that fact when they published plays. Several of Shakespeare's plays were performed before the sovereign, and Shakespeare himself undoubtedly acted in some of these plays.

References for Further Reading

Many readers will want suggestions for further reading about Shakespeare and his times. The literature in this field is enormous but a few references will serve as guides to further study. A simple and useful little book is Gerald Sanders, *A Shakespeare Primer* (New York, 1950). *A Companion to Shakespeare Studies* edited by Harley Granville-Barker and G. B. Harrison (Cambridge, Eng., 1934) is a valuable guide. More detailed but still not too voluminous to be confusing is Hazelton Spencer, *The Art and Life of William Shakespeare* (New York, 1940) which, like Sanders' handbook, contains a brief annotated list of useful books on various aspects of the subject. The most detailed and scholarly work providing complete factual information about Shakespeare is Sir Edmund Chambers, *William Shakespeare: A Study of Facts and Problems* (2 vols., Oxford, 1930). For detailed, factual information about the Elizabethan and seventeenth-century stages, the definitive reference works are Sir Edmund Chambers, *The Elizabethan Stage* (4 vols., Oxford, 1923) and Gerald E. Bentley, *The Jacobean and Caroline Stage* (5 vols., Oxford, 1941–1956). Alfred Harbage, *Shakespeare's Audience* (New York, 1941) and Martin Holmes, *Shakespeare's Public* (London, 1960) throw light on the nature and tastes of the customers for whom Elizabethan dramatists wrote.

Although specialists disagree about details of stage construction, the reader will find essential information in John C. Adams, *The Globe Playhouse: Its Design and Equipment* (Barnes & Noble, 1961). A model of the Globe playhouse by Dr. Adams is on permanent exhibition in the Folger Shakespeare Library in Washington, D.C. An excellent description of the architecture of the Globe is Irwin Smith, *Shakespeare's Globe Playhouse: A Modern Reconstruction in Text and Scale Drawings Based upon the Reconstruction of the Globe by John Cranford Adams* (New York, 1956). Another recent study of the physical characteristics of the Globe is C. Walter Hodges, *The Globe Restored* (London, 1953). A. M. Nagler's *Shakespeare's Stage* (New Haven, Conn., 1958) is a lucid synthesis of available information on the physical conditions in theatres of Shakespeare's age. An easily read history of the early theatres is J. Q. Adams, *Shakespearean Playhouses: A History of English Theatres from the Beginnings to the Restoration* (Boston, 1917).

The following titles on theatrical history will provide information about Shakespeare's plays in later periods: Alfred Harbage, *Theatre for Shakespeare* (Toronto, 1955); Esther Cloudman Dunn, *Shakespeare in America* (New York, 1939); George C. D. Odell, *Shakespeare from Betterton to Irving* (2 vols., London, 1921); Arthur Colby Sprague, *Shakespeare and the Actors: The Stage Business in His Plays (1660–1905)* (Cambridge, Mass., 1944) and *Shakespearian Players and Performances* (Cambridge, Mass., 1953); Leslie Hotson, *The Commonwealth and Restoration Stage* (Cambridge, Mass., 1928); Alwin Thaler, *Shakspere to Sheridan: A Book About the Theatre of Yesterday and To-day* (Cambridge, Mass., 1922); Ernest Bradlee Watson, *Sheridan to Robertson: A Study of the 19th-Century London Stage* (Cambridge, Mass., 1926). Enid Welsford, *The Court Masque* (Cambridge, Mass., 1927) is an excellent study of the characteristics of this form of entertainment.

The question of the authenticity of Shakespeare's plays arouses perennial attention. A book that demolishes the notion of hidden cryptograms in the plays is William F. Friedman and Elizebeth S. Friedman, *The Shakespearean Ciphers Examined* (New York, 1957). A succinct account of the various absurdities advanced to suggest the authorship of a multitude of candidates other than Shakespeare will be found in R. C. Churchill, *Shakespeare and His Betters* (Bloomington, Ind., 1959) and Frank W. Wadsworth, *The Poacher from Stratford: A Partial Account of the Controversy over the Authorship of Shakespeare's Plays* (Berkeley, Calif., 1958). An essay on the curious notions in the writings of the anti-Shakespeareans is that by Louis B. Wright, "The Anti-Shakespeare Industry and the Growth of Cults," *The Virginia Quarterly Review*, XXXV (1959), 289–303.

Harley Granville-Barker, *Prefaces to Shakespeare* (5 vols., London, 1927–1948) provides stimulating critical discussion of the plays. An older classic of criticism is Andrew C. Bradley, *Shakespearean Tragedy: Lectures on Hamlet, Othello, King Lear, Macbeth* (London, 1904), which is now available in an inexpensive reprint (New York, 1955). Thomas M. Parrott, *Shakespearean Comedy* (New York, 1949) is scholarly and readable. Shakespeare's dramatizations of English history are examined in E. M. W. Tillyard, *Shakespeare's History Plays* (London, 1948), and Lily Bess Campbell, *Shakespeare's "Histories," Mirrors of Elizabethan Policy* (San Marino, Calif., 1947) contains a more technical discussion of the same subject.

Reprints of some of the sources for Shakespeare's plays can be found in *Shakespeare's Library* (2 vols., 1850), edited by John Payne Collier, and *The Shakespeare Classics* (12 vols., 1907–1926), edited by Israel Gollancz. Geoffrey Bullough is the editor of a new series of volumes reprinting the sources, two volumes of which are in print: *Narrative and Dramatic Sources of Shakespeare. Volume 1. Early Comedies, Poems, and Romeo and Juliet* (New York, 1957); *Volume 2. The Comedies, 1597–1603* (New York, 1958). For discussion of Shakespeare's use of his sources see Kenneth Muir, *Shakespeare's Sources: Comedies and Tragedies* (London, 1957). Thomas M. Cranfill has recently edited a facsimile reprint of *Riche His Farewell to Military Profession* (1581), which contains stories probably used by Shakespeare for several of his plays.

Sir Edmund Chambers' thoughtful comment on *The Tempest* is found in his *Shakespeare: A Survey* (London, 1925), now available in a paperback version. Rudyard Kipling's letter to the *Spectator* was reprinted in *A Book of Homage to Shakespeare* (Oxford, 1916) and also appears in a booklet by Ashley H. Thorndike, *How Shakespeare Came to Write The Tempest* (New York, 1916). Thorndike's sprightly introduction is itself a stimulating essay. For an indication of Shakespeare's knowledge of the sea and seamanship illustrated in *The Tempest,* see L. G. Carr Laughton, "The Navy: Ships and Sailors," in *Shakespeare's England* (Oxford, 1925), I, 140–169. Chambers, *William Shakespeare: A Study of Facts and Problems* (Oxford, 1930) I, 490–491, lists the more significant books and articles on the sources of *The Tempest* and on Shakespeare's attitude toward the New World, topics which occupied the attention of scholars a few decades ago. A more recent and extensive discussion of the various themes treated in *The Tempest* is to be found in the introduction to the New Arden edition of the play, edited by Frank Kermode (London, 1954).

Interesting pictures as well as new information about Shakespeare will be found in F. E. Halliday, *Shakespeare, a Pictorial Biography* (London, 1956). Allardyce Nicoll, *The Elizabethans* (Cambridge, Eng., 1957) contains a variety of illustrations.

A brief, clear, and accurate account of Tudor history is S. T. Bindoff, *The Tudors,* in the Penguin series. A readable general history is G. M. Trevelyan, *The History of England,* first published in 1926 and available in many editions. G. M. Trevelyan, *English Social History,* first published in 1942 and also available in many editions, provides fascinating information about England in all periods. Sir John Neale, *Queen Elizabeth* (London, 1934) is the best study of the great Queen. Various aspects of life in the Elizabethan period are treated in Louis B. Wright, *Middle-Class Culture in Elizabethan England* (Chapel Hill, N. C., 1935; reprinted by Cornell University Press, 1958). *Shakespeare's England: An Account of the Life and Manners of His Age,* edited by Sidney Lee and C. T. Onions (2 vols., Oxford, 1916) provides a large amount of information on many aspects of life in the Elizabethan period. Additional detail will be found in Muriel St. C. Byrne, *Elizabethan Life in Town and Country* (Barnes & Noble, 1961).

The Folger Shakespeare Library is currently publishing a series of illustrated pamphlets on various aspects of English life in the sixteenth and seventeenth centuries. The following titles are available: Dorothy E. Mason, *Music in Elizabethan England;* Craig R.

Thompson, *The English Church in the Sixteenth Century;* Louis B. Wright, *Shakespeare's Theatre and the Dramatic Tradition;* Giles E. Dawson, *The Life of William Shakespeare;* Virginia A. LaMar, *English Dress in the Age of Shakespeare;* Craig R. Thompson, *The Bible in English, 1525–1611;* Craig R. Thompson, *Schools in Tudor England;* Craig R. Thompson, *Universities in Tudor England;* Lilly C. Stone, *English Sports and Recreations;* and Conyers Read, *The Government of England under Elizabeth.*

Names of the Actors

Alonso, King of Naples.
Sebastian, his brother.
Prospero, the right Duke of Milan.
Antonio, his brother, the usurping Duke of Milan.
Ferdinand, son to the King of Naples.
Gonzalo, an honest old counselor.
Adrian and *Francisco,* lords.
Caliban, a savage and deformed slave.
Trinculo, a jester.
Stephano, a drunken butler.
Master of a ship.
Boatswain.
Mariners.

Miranda, daughter to *Prospero.*
Ariel, an airy spirit.
Iris,
Ceres,
Juno, } [spirits].
Nymphs,
Reapers,

[Other *Spirits* serving *Prospero.*]

THE SCENE: [*A ship at sea; afterwards*] an uninhabited island.

xxxviii

THE TEMPEST

ACT I

I. i. Alonso, King of Naples; his brother, Sebastian; Antonio, who has usurped the dukedom of Milan; and their retainers are on board a ship which is endangered by a wild storm. As the scene ends, the ship seems about to sink and all fear they are lost.

━━━━━━━━━━━━━━

3. Good: colloquial for "my good fellow"; **fall to't yarely:** do it speedily.

6. Yare: yarely; as in 1. 3; **Tend:** attend; hearken.

7-8. Blow . . . wind: (addressing the storm); **if room enough:** i.e., if we are far enough from shore not to run aground.

ACT I

Scene I. [A ship at sea.]

A tempestuous noise of thunder and lightning heard.
Enter a Shipmaster and a Boatswain.

Mast. Boatswain!
Boats. Here, master. What cheer?
Mast. Good, speak to the mariners; fall to't yarely,
or we run ourselves aground! Bestir, bestir!   *Exit.*

Enter Mariners.

Boats. Heigh, my hearts! Cheerly, cheerly, my   5
hearts! Yare, yare! Take in the topsail! Tend to the
master's whistle! Blow till thou burst thy wind, if
room enough!

Enter Alonso, Sebastian, Antonio, Ferdinand,
Gonzalo, and others.

Alon. Good boatswain, have care. Where's the master? Play the men.   10

I

16. **cares:** a singular verb with a plural subject was common in Elizabethan usage.

28-30. **Methinks . . . gallows:** proverbial: "He that is born to be hanged shall never be drowned." The Elizabethans believed that the combination of the four humors hot, cold, moist, and dry—the "complexion"—determined temperament; **complexion** is used in this sense.

35. **Bring . . . course:** heave her to with only the mainsail set. The intention is to keep the ship as stable as possible to avoid being blown onto land.

36. **they:** i.e., the passengers.

37. **office:** function; i.e., the noise of calling orders to work the ship.

Boats. I pray now, keep below.

Ant. Where is the master, bos'n?

Boats. Do you not hear him? You mar our labor. Keep your cabins: you do assist the storm!

Gon. Nay, good, be patient. 15

Boats. When the sea is. Hence! What cares these roarers for the name of king? To cabin! Silence! Trouble us not!

Gon. Good, yet remember whom thou hast aboard.

Boats. None that I more love than myself. You are 20 a counselor: if you can command these elements to silence and work the peace of the present, we will not hand a rope more; use your authority. If you cannot, give thanks you have lived so long, and make yourself ready in your cabin for the mischance of 25 the hour, if it so hap.—Cheerly, good hearts!—Out of our way, I say. *Exit.*

Gon. I have great comfort from this fellow. Methinks he hath no drowning mark upon him; his complexion is perfect gallows. Stand fast, good Fate, to 30 his hanging! Make the rope of his destiny our cable, for our own doth little advantage. If he be not born to be hanged, our case is miserable. *Exeunt.*

[Re-]*enter Boatswain.*

Boats. Down with the topmast! Yare! Lower, lower! Bring her to try with main course! (*A cry within.*) 35 A plague upon this howling! They are louder than the weather or our office.

46. **warrant him for:** i.e., stand surety that he will not drown.

49. **Lay her ahold, ahold! Set her two courses:** "bring her close to the wind. Spread her foresail as well as her mainsail." The ship is dangerously close to the land and the boatswain's orders are designed to prevent running aground.

50. **Lay her off:** move her away from shore.

57. **merely:** completely.

59. **wide-chopped:** wide-jawed; i.e., big-mouthed.

61. **The washing of ten tides:** a reference to the manner of execution of pirates, who were hanged at the low-tide line and allowed to remain through several tides.

Long Heath.
From Rembert Dodoens, *A New Herbal* (1578).

Enter Sebastian, Antonio, and Gonzalo.

Yet again? What do you here? Shall we give o'er and
drown? Have you a mind to sink?

Seb. A pox o' your throat, you bawling, blasphe- 40
mous, incharitable dog!

Boats. Work you then.

Ant. Hang, cur, hang, you whoreson, insolent
noisemaker! We are less afraid to be drowned than
thou art. 45

Gon. I'll warrant him for drowning, though the
ship were no stronger than a nutshell and as leaky as
an unstanched wench.

Boats. Lay her ahold, ahold! Set her two courses!
Off to sea again! Lay her off! 50

Enter Mariners, wet.

Mariners. All lost! To prayers, to prayers! All lost!
                                  [*Exeunt.*]

Boats. What, must our mouths be cold?

Gon. The King and Prince at prayers! Let's assist
    them,

For our case is as theirs. 55

Seb.   I am out of patience.

Ant. We are merely cheated of our lives by drunk-
    ards.

This wide-chopped rascal—would thou mightst lie
    drowning 60

The washing of ten tides!

Gon.   He'll be hanged yet,

64. gape at wid'st to glut him: open its mouth wide to swallow him.

72-3. long heath, brown furze: two varieties of worthless plants, heather and gorse, which grow on uncultivated ground.

<hr/>

I. ii. Miranda accuses her father, Prospero, of causing the storm. Prospero assures her that no one aboard the ship is harmed and explains his motives. He tells her that he is the rightful Duke of Milan but that his brother Antonio usurped his dukedom and expelled him. Though he and Miranda had been set afloat in a rotten ship they finally landed on the island, where Fortune has now brought their enemies into Prospero's power.

Charming Miranda to sleep, Prospero questions Ariel, a spirit in his service, about the tempest. Both ship and passengers are safe and the royal party is dispersed about the island. For this service, Ariel begs his freedom, but Prospero reminds him that he must serve a while longer in return for being rescued from imprisonment by the witch Sycorax. Sycorax's son, Caliban, appears when summoned, uttering curses against Prospero; he resents serving Prospero but cannot resist his power.

Ariel lures Ferdinand, son of the King of Naples, to the spot, and Miranda and Ferdinand fall in love at first sight. Prospero secretly approves but resolves to test the young man.

<hr/>

4. welkin: sky.

6. brave: splendid; gallant.

4

Though every drop of water swear against it
And gape at wid'st to glut him.

    A confused noise within: "Mercy on us—   65
    We split, we split!—Farewell, my wife and chil-
      dren!—
    Farewell, brother!—We split, we split, we split!"
                              [*Exit Boatswain.*]

    Ant. Let's all sink with the King.
    Seb.   Let's take leave of him.   70
           Exeunt [*Antonio and Sebastian*].
    Gon. Now would I give a thousand furlongs of sea
for an acre of barren ground—long heath, brown
furze, anything. The wills above be done, but I would
fain die a dry death.

                                    Exit.

Scene II. [The island. Before Prospero's cell.]

Enter Prospero and Miranda.

    Mir. If by your art, my dearest father, you have
Put the wild waters in this roar, allay them.
The sky, it seems, would pour down stinking pitch
But that the sea, mounting to the welkin's cheek,
Dashes the fire out. O, I have suffered   5
With those that I saw suffer! a brave vessel
(Who had no doubt some noble creature in her)
Dashed all to pieces! O, the cry did knock

13. **fraughting souls within her:** humans borne by her. "Fraught" is an obsolete word for "freight."

15. **amazement:** overwhelming dismay.

22. **more better:** double comparatives are not uncommon in Elizabethan English.

23-4. **master of a full poor cell,/And thy no greater father:** owner of only a humble cell and a father of no greater worth than that.

26. **meddle:** mix.

32. **wrack:** wreck.

33. **very virtue of compassion in thee:** i.e., the depths of your compassion.

36. **perdition:** loss.

37. **Betid:** befallen.

From Guillaume de la Perriére, *La Morosophie* (1553).

Against my very heart! Poor souls, they perished!
Had I been any god of power, I would   10
Have sunk the sea within the earth or ere
It should the good ship so have swallowed and
The fraughting souls within her.

   Pros.   Be collected.
No more amazement. Tell your piteous heart   15
There's no harm done.

   Mir.   O, woe the day!

   Pros.   No harm.
I have done nothing but in care of thee,
Of thee my dear one, thee my daughter, who   20
Art ignorant of what thou art, naught knowing
Of whence I am; nor that I am more better
Than Prospero, master of a full poor cell,
And thy no greater father.

   Mir.   More to know   25
Did never meddle with my thoughts.

   Pros.   'Tis time
I should inform thee farther. Lend thy hand
And pluck my magic garment from me. So,

                    [*Takes off his magic robe.*]
Lie there, my art. Wipe thou thine eyes; have com-   30
    fort.
The direful spectacle of the wrack, which touched
The very virtue of compassion in thee,
I have with such provision in mine art
So safely ordered that there is no soul—   35
No, not so much perdition as an hair
Betid to any creature in the vessel

43. **bootless:** unprofitable; useless.
50. **Out:** quite.
57. **remembrance warrants:** memory certifies.
61. **backward:** past.

Which thou heardst cry, which thou sawst sink. Sit
    down;
For thou must now know farther.   40
  Mir.   You have often
Begun to tell me what I am, but stopped
And left me to a bootless inquisition,
Concluding, "Stay! Not yet."
  Pros.   The hour's now come;   45
The very minute bids thee ope thine ear.
Obey, and be attentive. Canst thou remember
A time before we came unto this cell?
I do not think thou canst, for then thou wast not
Out three years old.   50
  Mir.   Certainly, sir, I can.
  Pros. By what? By any other house or person?
Of anything the image tell me that
Hath kept with thy remembrance.
  Mir.   'Tis far off,   55
And rather like a dream than an assurance
That my remembrance warrants. Had I not
Four or five women once that tended me?
  Pros. Thou hadst, and more, Miranda. But how is it
That this lives in thy mind? What seest thou else   60
In the dark backward and abysm of time?
If thou rememb'rest aught ere thou camest here,
How thou camest here thou mayst.
  Mir.   But that I do not.
  Pros. Twelve year since, Miranda, twelve year   65
    since,
Thy father was the Duke of Milan and
A prince of power.

70. **piece:** masterpiece.

73. **no worse issued:** born of no worse parentage.

79. **holp:** helped.

81. **teen that I have turned you to:** trouble I have made you recall.

82. **from:** gone from.

88. **seignories:** dominions.

97. **Being once perfected:** once having mastered.

99. **trash for overtopping:** slow his advance. A hunting dog was "trashed" (slowed by an attached weight) to check his speed when he began to outrun the rest of the pack.

Mir.   Sir, are not you my father?

Pros. Thy mother was a piece of virtue, and 70
She said thou wast my daughter; and thy father
Was Duke of Milan; and his only heir
A princess—no worse issued.

Mir.   O the heavens!
What foul play had we that we came from thence? 75
Or blessed was't we did?

Pros.   Both, both, my girl!
By foul play, as thou sayst, were we heaved thence,
But blessedly holp hither.

Mir.   O, my heart bleeds 80
To think o' the teen that I have turned you to,
Which is from my remembrance! Please you, farther.

Pros. My brother, and thy uncle, called Antonio—
I pray thee mark me—that a brother should
Be so perfidious!—he whom next thyself 85
Of all the world I loved, and to him put
The manage of my state, as at that time
Through all the seignories it was the first,
And Prospero the prime duke, being so reputed
In dignity, and for the liberal arts 90
Without a parallel; those being all my study,
The government I cast upon my brother
And to my state grew stranger, being transported
And rapt in secret studies—thy false uncle—
Dost thou attend me? 95

Mir.   Sir, most heedfully.

Pros. Being once perfected how to grant suits,
How to deny them, who t' advance, and who
To trash for overtopping, new-created

101-2. having both the key/Of officer and office: i.e., having control over both state offices and appointment of men to fill them. The imagery is from music.

103-5. that: so that; **now he was/The ivy which had hid my princely trunk/And sucked my verdure out on't:** that is, he finally obscured me as head of state and, though previously dependent upon me for support, now stole my power; **on't:** of it.

109. closeness: retirement; a life of seclusion.

110-11. but by being so retired,/O'erprized all popular rate: had it not been so removed from common knowledge, would have been prized more highly than anything else.

112-13. my trust,/Like a good parent: a reference to the proverb "Trust is the mother of deceit."

116. sans: without; **lorded:** given lordly power.

122. out o' the substitution: as a result of being made the Duke's deputy.

123-24. executing the outward face of royalty/With all prerogative: performing royalty's functions with the full power attendant thereto.

127. screen: i.e., barrier.

129. needs will be: i.e., feels he must be.

130. Absolute Milan: the legal Duke of Milan.

The creatures that were mine, I say, or changed 'em,   100
Or else new-formed 'em; having both the key
Of officer and office, set all hearts i' the state
To what tune pleased his ear, that now he was
The ivy which had hid my princely trunk
And sucked my verdure out on't. Thou attendst not!   105
    Mir. O, good sir, I do.
     Pros.   I pray thee mark me.
I thus neglecting worldly ends, all dedicated
To closeness, and the bettering of my mind
With that which, but by being so retired,   110
O'erprized all popular rate, in my false brother
Awaked an evil nature, and my trust,
Like a good parent, did beget of him
A falsehood in its contrary as great
As my trust was, which had indeed no limit,   115
A confidence sans bound. He being thus lorded,
Not only with what my revenue yielded
But what my power might else exact, like one
Who having unto truth, by telling of it,
Made such a sinner of his memory   120
To credit his own lie, he did believe
He was indeed the Duke, out o' the substitution
And executing the outward face of royalty
With all prerogative. Hence his ambition growing—
Dost thou hear?   125
    Mir.   Your tale, sir, would cure deafness.
    Pros. To have no screen between this part he
       played
And him he played it for, he needs will be
Absolute Milan. Me (poor man) my library   130

131. **temporal:** worldly.

133. **dry:** thirsty; avid.

139. **condition:** i.e., the details of his agreement with the King of Naples; **event:** outcome.

141. **might be:** i.e., could possibly be.

148. **in lieu o' the premises:** in return for stipulated money payments (the terms premised in their agreement).

150. **presently:** at once; **extirpate:** root out.

153. **levied:** mustered.

160. **hint:** suitable occasion.

Was dukedom large enough! Of temporal royalties
He thinks me now incapable; confederates
(So dry he was for sway) with the King of Naples
To give him annual tribute, do him homage,
Subject his coronet to his crown, and bend   135
The dukedom yet unbowed (alas, poor Milan!)
To most ignoble stooping.

   Mir.   O the heavens!

   Pros. Mark his condition, and the event; then tell
    me   140
If this might be a brother.

   Mir.   I should sin
To think but nobly of my grandmother.
Good wombs have borne bad sons.

   Pros.   Now the condition. 145
This King of Naples, being an enemy
To me inveterate, hearkens my brother's suit;
Which was, that he, in lieu o' the premises,
Of homage and I know not how much tribute,
Should presently extirpate me and mine   150
Out of the dukedom and confer fair Milan,
With all the honors, on my brother. Whereon,
A treacherous army levied, one midnight
Fated to the purpose, did Antonio open
The gates of Milan; and, i' the dead of darkness, 155
The ministers for the purpose hurried thence
Me and thy crying self.

   Mir.   Alack, for pity!
I, not rememb'ring how I cried out then,
Will cry it o'er again. It is a hint   160
That wrings mine eyes to't.

164. **now's upon's:** now is upon us.

165. **were:** would be; **impertinent:** i.e., not pertinent; irrelevant.

172. **With colors fairer painted their foul ends:** disguised their evil purposes with fair pretenses.

175. **butt:** old tub.

177. **hoist:** hoisted; i.e., put us aboard.

180. **Did us but loving wrong:** i.e., the winds demonstrated pity by sighing as they buffeted Prospero and Miranda.

186. **decked:** sprinkled, a dialectal usage.

188. **undergoing stomach:** courage to endure.

Pros. Hear a little further,
And then I'll bring thee to the present business
Which now's upon's; without the which this story
Were most impertinent. 165
    Mir. Wherefore did they not
That hour destroy us?
    Pros. Well demanded, wench.
My tale provokes that question. Dear, they durst not,
So dear the love my people bore me; nor set 170
A mark so bloody on the business; but
With colors fairer painted their foul ends.
In few, they hurried us aboard a bark,
Bore us some leagues to sea; where they prepared
A rotten carcass of a butt, not rigged, 175
Nor tackle, sail, nor mast; the very rats
Instinctively have quit it. There they hoist us,
To cry to the sea, that roared to us; to sigh
To the winds, whose pity, sighing back again,
Did us but loving wrong. 180
    Mir. Alack, what trouble
Was I then to you!
    Pros. O, a cherubin
Thou wast that did preserve me! Thou didst smile,
Infused with a fortitude from heaven, 185
When I have decked the sea with drops full salt,
Under my burden groaned; which raised in me
An undergoing stomach, to bear up
Against what should ensue.
    Mir. How came we ashore? 190
    Pros. By providence divine.
Some food we had, and some fresh water, that

197. **steaded much:** been very useful; **of his gentleness:** out of his kindness.

207. **princess:** princesses.

208. **vainer hours:** hours more uselessly spent.

217. **my zenith:** the height of my fortunes.

219. **omit:** neglect.

222. **give it way:** allow it to have its way.

A noble Neapolitan, Gonzalo,
Out of his charity, who being then appointed
Master of this design, did give us, with   195
Rich garments, linens, stuffs, and necessaries
Which since have steaded much. So, of his gentleness,
Knowing I loved my books, he furnished me
From mine own library with volumes that
I prize above my dukedom.   200
    Mir.   Would I might
But ever see that man!
    Pros.   Now I arise.
Sit still, and hear the last of our sea-sorrow.
Here in this island we arrived; and here   205
Have I, thy schoolmaster, made thee more profit
Than other princess can, that have more time
For vainer hours, and tutors not so careful.
    Mir. Heavens thank you for't! And now I pray
      you, sir,—   210
For still 'tis beating in my mind,—your reason
For raising this sea-storm?
    Pros.   Know thus far forth.
By accident most strange, bountiful Fortune
(Now my dear lady) hath mine enemies   215
Brought to this shore; and by my prescience
I find my zenith doth depend upon
A most auspicious star, whose influence
If now I court not, but omit, my fortunes
Will ever after droop. Here cease more questions.   220
Thou art inclined to sleep. 'Tis a good dullness,
And give it way. I know thou canst not choose.
                     [Miranda sleeps.]

225. **Grave:** reverend.

228. **task:** tax.

229. **all his quality:** all his kind; i.e., all his associate spirits.

231. **to point:** exactly.

233. **beak:** prow.

234. **waist:** the middle part of the upper deck of a ship, between the quarterdeck and the forecastle.

235. **flamed amazement:** burned so as to amaze the beholders; see **amazement** at l. 15.

237. **distinctly:** severally; i.e., in each spot named simultaneously.

245. **constant:** well-balanced; **coil:** uproar.

248. **fever of the mad:** fit of madness.

Jove with thunderbolts and lightning.
From Vincenzo Cartari, *Imagini de gli dei delli antichi* (1615).

Come away, servant, come! I am ready now.
Approach, my Ariel. Come!

Enter Ariel.

  Ariel. All hail, great master! Grave sir, hail! I come 225
To answer thy best pleasure; be't to fly,
To swim, to dive into the fire, to ride
On the curled clouds. To thy strong bidding task
Ariel and all his quality.
    Pros.   Hast thou, spirit,   230
Performed to point the tempest that I bade thee?
  Ariel. To every article.
I boarded the King's ship. Now on the beak,
Now in the waist, the deck, in every cabin,
I flamed amazement. Sometime I'ld divide   235
And burn in many places; on the topmast,
The yards, and bowsprit would I flame distinctly,
Then meet and join. Jove's lightnings, the precursors
O' the dreadful thunderclaps, more momentary
And sight-outrunning were not. The fire and cracks   240
Of sulphurous roaring the most mighty Neptune
Seem to besiege and make his bold waves tremble;
Yea, his dread trident shake.
    Pros.   My brave spirit!
Who was so firm, so constant, that this coil   245
Would not infect his reason?
    Ariel.   Not a soul
But felt a fever of the mad and played
Some tricks of desperation. All but mariners

260. **sustaining garments:** clothing, which buoyed them up in the water.

266. **arms in this sad knot:** i.e., with arms folded.

273. **still-vexed:** perpetually storm-ridden; **Bermoothes:** Bermudas.

278. **float:** sea.

Neptune
From Andrea Alciati, *Emblemata* (1577).

Plunged in the foaming brine and quit the vessel, 250
Then all afire with me. The King's son Ferdinand,
With hair up-staring (then like reeds, not hair),
Was the first man that leapt; cried "Hell is empty,
And all the devils are here!"
    Pros.   Why, that's my spirit! 255
But was not this nigh shore?
    Ariel.   Close by, my master.
    Pros. But are they, Ariel, safe?
    Ariel.   Not a hair perished.
On their sustaining garments not a blemish, 260
But fresher than before; and as thou badest me,
In troops I have dispersed them 'bout the isle.
The King's son have I landed by himself,
Whom I left cooling of the air with sighs
In an odd angle of the isle, and sitting, 265
His arms in this sad knot.
    Pros.   Of the King's ship
The mariners say how thou hast disposed,
And all the rest o' the fleet.
    Ariel.   Safely in harbor 270
Is the King's ship; in the deep nook where once
Thou calledst me up at midnight to fetch dew
From the still-vexed Bermoothes, there she's hid;
The mariners all under hatches stowed,
Who, with a charm joined to their suff'red labor, 275
I have left asleep; and for the rest o' the fleet,
Which I dispersed, they all have met again,
And are upon the Mediterranean float
Bound sadly home for Naples,

286. **glasses:** hourglasses; hours.

287. **preciously:** i.e., so as to take the utmost advantage of each minute.

289. **pains:** painful tasks.

290. **remember:** remind.

299. **or . . . or:** either . . . or.

300. **bate:** abate; shorten his length of service.

Supposing that they saw the King's ship wracked   280
And his great person perish.

   Pros.   Ariel, thy charge
Exactly is performed; but there's more work.
What is the time o' the day?

   Ariel.   Past the mid season.   285

   Pros. At least two glasses. The time 'twixt six and now
Must by us both be spent most preciously.

   Ariel. Is there more toil? Since thou dost give me
    pains,
Let me remember thee what thou hast promised,   290
Which is not yet performed me.

   Pros.   How now? moody?
What is't thou canst demand?

   Ariel.   My liberty.

   Pros. Before the time be out? No more!   295

   Ariel.   I prithee,
Remember I have done thee worthy service,
Told thee no lies, made no mistakings, served
Without or grudge or grumblings. Thou didst promise
To bate me a full year.   300

   Pros.   Dost thou forget
From what a torment I did free thee?

   Ariel.   No.

   Pros. Thou dost; and thinkst it much to tread the
    ooze   305
Of the salt deep,
To run upon the sharp wind of the North,
To do me business in the veins o' the earth
When it is baked with frost.

   Ariel.   I do not, sir.   310

312. **envy:** malice.

317. **Argier:** Algiers.

326. **blue-eyed:** i.e., her eyes were discolored by blue shadows.

332. **grand hests:** important commands.

333. **ministers:** agents; i.e., other spirits under Sycorax's domination.

338. **vent:** utter.

340. **mill wheels strike:** a reference to the contrivance on a mill wheel that struck as it turned against the grain hopper to shake the grain to the grinding surfaces.

Pros. Thou liest, malignant thing! Hast thou forgot
The foul witch Sycorax, who with age and envy
Was grown into a hoop? Hast thou forgot her?

   Ariel. No, sir.

   Pros.   Thou hast. Where was she born?   315
      Speak! Tell me!

   Ariel. Sir, in Argier.

   Pros.   O, was she so? I must
Once in a month recount what thou hast been,
Which thou forgetst. This damned witch Sycorax,   320
For mischiefs manifold, and sorceries terrible
To enter human hearing, from Argier
Thou knowst was banished. For one thing she did
They would not take her life. Is not this true?

   Ariel. Ay, sir.   325

   Pros. This blue-eyed hag was hither brought with
      child
And here was left by the sailors. Thou, my slave,
As thou reportst thyself, wast then her servant;
And, for thou wast a spirit too delicate   330
To act her earthy and abhorred commands,
Refusing her grand hests, she did confine thee,
By help of her more potent ministers,
And in her most unmitigable rage,
Into a cloven pine; within which rift   335
Imprisoned thou didst painfully remain
A dozen years; within which space she died
And left thee there; where thou didst vent thy
      groans
As fast as mill wheels strike. Then was this island   340
(Save for the son that she did litter here,

356. **his:** its.

359. **correspondent:** responsive; submissive.

360. **do my spriting gently:** perform a spirit's duties for you graciously.

A freckled whelp, hag-born) not honored with
A human shape.
   Ariel.   Yes, Caliban, her son.
   Pros. Dull thing, I say so! he, that Caliban   345
Whom now I keep in service. Thou best knowst
What torment I did find thee in. Thy groans
Did make wolves howl and penetrate the breasts
Of ever-angry bears. It was a torment
To lay upon the damned, which Sycorax   350
Could not again undo. It was mine art,
When I arrived and heard thee, that made gape
The pine, and let thee out.
   Ariel.   I thank thee, master.
   Pros. If thou more murmurst, I will rend an oak   355
And peg thee in his knotty entrails till
Thou hast howled away twelve winters.
   Ariel.   Pardon, master.
I will be correspondent to command
And do my spriting gently.   360
   Pros.   Do so; and after two days
I will discharge thee.
   Ariel.   That's my noble master!
What shall I do? Say what! What shall I do?
   Pros. Go make thyself like a nymph o' the sea. Be 365
    subject
To no sight but thine and mine; invisible
To every eyeball else. Go take this shape
And hither come in't. Go! Hence with diligence!
                           Exit [*Ariel*].
Awake, dear heart, awake! Thou hast slept well.   370
Awake!

380. **miss:** manage without.

387. **When:** i.e., when are you coming forth?

388. **quaint:** clever.

394. **wicked:** baneful; poisonous.

396. **southwest:** southwest wind; i.e., a hot, moist wind, laden with infection.

Mir. The strangeness of your story put
Heaviness in me.

Pros.   Shake it off. Come on.
We'll visit Caliban, my slave, who never   375
Yields us kind answer.

Mir.   'Tis a villain, sir,
I do not love to look on.

Pros.   But as 'tis,
We cannot miss him. He does make our fire,   380
Fetch in our wood, and serves in offices
That profit us. What, ho! slave! Caliban!
Thou earth, thou! Speak!

Cal. (Within)   There's wood enough within.

Pros. Come forth, I say! There's other business for 385
     thee.
Come, thou tortoise! When?

Enter Ariel like a water nymph.

Fine apparition! My quaint Ariel,
Hark in thine ear.

Ariel.   My lord, it shall be done.   *Exit.* 390

Pros. Thou poisonous slave, got by the Devil him-
     self
Upon thy wicked dam, come forth!

Enter Caliban.

Cal. As wicked dew as e'er my mother brushed
With raven's feather from unwholesome fen   395
Drop on you both! A southwest blow on ye
And blister you all o'er!

400. **urchins:** goblins. Hedgehogs, also known as **urchins**, were considered by some authorities on witchcraft to be shapes frequently assumed by witches' familiars. See also II. ii. 5 and 10.

401. **vast:** immense expanse. Shakespeare sometimes pictures night as an endless stretch of empty blackness, as in *Hamlet* I. ii. 210: "In the dead vast and middle of the night."

Pros. For this, be sure, tonight thou shalt have
  cramps,
Side-stitches that shall pen thy breath up; urchins   400
Shall, for that vast of night that they may work,
All exercise on thee; thou shalt be pinched
As thick as honeycomb, each pinch more stinging
Than bees that made 'em.

Cal.   I must eat my dinner.   405
This island's mine by Sycorax my mother,
Which thou takest from me. When thou camest first,
Thou strokedst me and made much of me; wouldst
  give me
Water with berries in't; and teach me how   410
To name the bigger light, and how the less,
That burn by day, and night; and then I loved thee
And showed thee all the qualities o' the isle,
The fresh springs, brine-pits, barren place and fertile.
Cursed be I that did so! All the charms   415
Of Sycorax—toads, beetles, bats light on you!
For I am all the subjects that you have,
Which first was mine own king; and here you sty me
In this hard rock, whiles you do keep from me
The rest o' the island.   420

Pros.   Thou most lying slave,
Whom stripes may move, not kindness! I have used
  thee
(Filth as thou art) with humane care, and lodged
  thee   425
In mine own cell till thou didst seek to violate
The honor of my child.

Cal. O ho, O ho! Would't had been done!

431-43. Some editors consider these lines too strong for Miranda and alter the Folio's speech prefix to "Prospero."

445. **red plague:** bubonic plague; **rid:** kill.

448. **thou'rt best:** you had better.

Thou didst prevent me; I had peopled else
This isle with Calibans.   430
  Mir.   Abhorred slave,
Which any print of goodness wilt not take,
Being capable of all ill! I pitied thee,
Took pains to make thee speak, taught thee each hour
One thing or other. When thou didst not, savage,   435
Know thine own meaning, but wouldst gabble like
A thing most brutish, I endowed thy purposes
With words that made them known. But thy vile race,
Though thou didst learn, had that in't which good
    natures   440
Could not abide to be with. Therefore wast thou
Deservedly confined into this rock, who hadst
Deserved more than a prison.
  Cal. You taught me language, and my profit on't
Is, I know how to curse. The red plague rid you   445
For learning me your language!
  Pros.   Hag-seed, hence!
Fetch us in fuel; and be quick, thou'rt best,
To answer other business. Shrugst thou, malice?
If thou neglectst or dost unwillingly   450
What I command, I'll rack thee with old cramps,
Fill all thy bones with aches, make thee roar
That beasts shall tremble at thy din.
  Cal.   No, pray thee.
[*Aside*] I must obey. His art is of such pow'r   455
It would control my dam's god, Setebos,
And make a vassal of him.
  Pros.   So, slave; hence!
                          Exit Caliban.

461. **Curtsied when you have:** i.e., when you have curtsied.

462. **whist:** hushed.

463. **featly:** nimbly or gracefully.

464. **burden:** refrain.

466. S.D. **dispersedly:** i.e., from several directions, as though sung by scattered spirits.

478. **passion:** storm of grief.

Enter Ferdinand; and Ariel, invisible,
playing and singing.

Ariel's song.

Come unto these yellow sands,
   And then take hands.   460
Curtsied when you have and kissed,
   The wild waves whist,
Foot it featly here and there;
And, sweet sprites, the burden bear.
   Hark, hark!   465

Burden dispersedly. Bow, wow!
   The watchdogs bark.

Burden dispersedly. Bow, wow!

  Ariel.   Hark, hark! I hear
       The strain of strutting chanticleer   470
         Cry, cock-a-diddle-dowe.

  Fer. Where should this music be? I' the air, or the
    earth?
It sounds no more; and sure it waits upon
Some god o' the island. Sitting on a bank,   475
Weeping again the King my father's wrack,
This music crept by me upon the waters,
Allaying both their fury and my passion
With its sweet air. Thence I have followed it,
Or it hath drawn me rather; but 'tis gone.   480
No, it begins again.

493. **owes:** possesses.
498. **brave:** handsome; splendid; see l. 6.
502. **something:** somewhat; **stained:** marred.

Ariel's song.

Full fathom five thy father lies;
　Of his bones are coral made;
Those are pearls that were his eyes;
　Nothing of him that doth fade　　　　　485
But doth suffer a sea-change
Into something rich and strange.
Sea nymphs hourly ring his knell:

Burden. Ding-dong.

　　Hark! now I hear them—Ding-dong bell.　　490

Fer. The ditty does remember my drowned father.
This is no mortal business, nor no sound
That the earth owes. I hear it now above me.
　Pros. The fringed curtains of thine eye advance
And say what thou seest yond.　　　　　495
　Mir.　　　　　　　What is't? a spirit?
Lord, how it looks about! Believe me, sir,
It carries a brave form. But 'tis a spirit.
　Pros. No, wench. It eats, and sleeps, and hath such
　　senses　　　　　500
As we have, such. This gallant which thou seest
Was in the wrack; and, but he's something stained
With grief (that's beauty's canker), thou mightst call
　　him
A goodly person. He hath lost his fellows　　　505
And strays about to find 'em.

510-11. **It goes on . . . /As my soul prompts it:** i.e., Miranda is attracted to Ferdinand, as Prospero has willed that she should be.

514-15. **Vouchsafe my pray'r/May know:** let my prayer prevail upon you to tell me.

517. **bear me:** conduct myself.

519. **maid:** i.e., mortal.

527. **single:** solitary.

529. **Naples:** the King of Naples. See **Absolute Milan** at l. 130.

530. **eyes, never since at ebb:** eyes that have never since ceased weeping.

536. **control thee:** correct your mistake (since they know the whereabouts of the true Duke of Milan).

Mir.   I might call him
A thing divine, for nothing natural
I ever saw so noble.
 Pros. [*Aside*]   It goes on, I see,   510
As my soul prompts it. Spirit, fine spirit! I'll free thee
Within two days for this.
 Fer.   Most sure, the goddess
On whom these airs attend! Vouchsafe my pray'r
May know if you remain upon this island,   515
And that you will some good instruction give
How I may bear me here. My prime request,
Which I do last pronounce, is (O you wonder!)
If you be maid or no?
 Mir.   No wonder, sir,   520
But certainly a maid.
 Fer.   My language? Heavens!
I am the best of them that speak this speech,
Were I but where 'tis spoken.
 Pros.   How? the best?   525
What wert thou if the King of Naples heard thee?
 Fer. A single thing, as I am now, that wonders
To hear thee speak of Naples. He does hear me;
And that he does I weep. Myself am Naples,
Who with mine eyes, never since at ebb, beheld   530
The King, my father, wracked.
 Mir.   Alack, for mercy!
 Fer. Yes, faith, and all his lords, the Duke of Milan
And his brave son being twain.
 Pros. [*Aside*]   The Duke of Milan   535
And his more braver daughter could control thee,
If now 'twere fit to do't. At the first sight

538. **changed:** exchanged.

540. **done yourself some wrong:** i.e., in speaking what is not the truth.

548. **Soft:** just a minute.

554. **owest:** ownest; see l. 493.

568. **entertainment:** treatment.

They have changed eyes. Delicate Ariel,
I'll set thee free for this!—A word, good sir.
I fear you have done yourself some wrong. A word! 540
   Mir. Why speaks my father so ungently? This
Is the third man that e'er I saw; the first
That e'er I sighed for. Pity move my father
To be inclined my way!
   Fer.   O, if a virgin, 545
And your affection not gone forth, I'll make you
The Queen of Naples.
   Pros.   Soft, sir! one word more.
[*Aside*] They are both in either's pow'rs. But this
   swift business 550
I must uneasy make, lest too light winning
Make the prize light.—One word more! I charge thee
That thou attend me. Thou dost here usurp
The name thou owest not, and hast put thyself
Upon this island as a spy, to win it 555
From me, the lord on't.
   Fer.   No, as I am a man!
   Mir. There's nothing ill can dwell in such a temple.
If the ill spirit have so fair a house,
Good things will strive to dwell with't. 560
   Pros.   Follow me.—
Speak not you for him; he's a traitor.—Come!
I'll manacle thy neck and feet together;
Sea water shalt thou drink; thy food shall be
The fresh brook mussels, withered roots, and husks 565
Wherein the acorn cradled. Follow.
   Fer.   No.
I will resist such entertainment till

571. **Make not too rash a trial of him:** do not judge him too hastily.

572. **gentle, and not fearful:** a gentleman and not cowardly.

574. **My foot my tutor:** i.e., my inferior in years and judgment presuming to instruct me.

577. **from thy ward:** abandon your fighting stance (addressed to Ferdinand).

580. **Beseech you:** please.

591. **affections:** tastes.

595. **nerves:** i.e., strength.

598. **spirits:** energies.

Mine enemy has more power.

He draws, and is charmed from moving.

Mir.   O dear father,   570
Make not too rash a trial of him, for
He's gentle, and not fearful.

Pros.   What, I say,
My foot my tutor?—Put thy sword up, traitor!
Who makest a show but darest not strike, thy con-   575
    science
Is so possessed with guilt. Come, from thy ward!
For I can here disarm thee with this stick
And make thy weapon drop.

Mir.   Beseech you, father!   580

Pros. Hence! Hang not on my garments.

Mir.   Sir, have pity.
I'll be his surety.

Pros.   Silence! One word more
Shall make me chide thee, if not hate thee. What,   585
An advocate for an impostor? Hush!
Thou thinkst there is no more such shapes as he,
Having seen but him and Caliban. Foolish wench!
To the most of men this is a Caliban,
And they to him are angels.   590

Mir.   My affections
Are then most humble. I have no ambition
To see a goodlier man.

Pros.   Come on, obey!
Thy nerves are in their infancy again   595
And have no vigor in them.

Fer.   So they are.
My spirits, as in a dream, are all bound up.

My father's loss, the weakness which I feel,
The wrack of all my friends, nor this man's threats   600
To whom I am subdued, are but light to me,
Might I but through my prison once a day
Behold this maid. All corners else o' the earth
Let liberty make use of; space enough
Have I in such a prison.   605

   Pros. [*Aside*]   It works. [*To Ferdinand*]
    Come on.—
Thou hast done well, fine Ariel! [*To Ferdinand*] Fol-
    low me.—
[*To Ariel*] Hark what thou else shalt do me.   610
   Mir.   Be of comfort.
My father's of a better nature, sir,
Than he appears by speech. This is unwonted
Which now came from him.

   Pros.   Thou shalt be as free   615
As mountain winds; but then exactly do
All points of my command.

   Ariel.   To the syllable.
   Pros. Come, follow.—Speak not for him.

               Exeunt.

THE TEMPEST

ACT II

II. i. Gonzalo, a noble old counselor, attempts to console Alonso, who is disconsolate at the loss of his son. The other lords are sarcastic at Gonzalo's expense, and Alonso regrets having married his daughter to the King of Tunis, for they were returning thence when the storm destroyed their ship. The invisible Ariel lulls all to sleep except Sebastian and Antonio, and the latter convinces Sebastian that if he kills his brother Alonso he may have the kingdom of Naples. As they draw their swords, Ariel awakens Gonzalo and the King is saved. The two would-be murderers claim to have drawn their swords to fend off a wild beast. They all leave their present spot and continue the search for Alonso's son.

|||||||||||||||||||||||||||||||||||||||

1. **merry:** cheerful.
3. **hint:** occasion; see I. ii. 160.
5. **some merchant:** some merchant ship; **the merchant:** the shipowner.
12. **visitor:** consoler (Gonzalo).
16. **Tell:** count how many times it strikes.
17. **entertained:** that is, accepted graciously.

ACT II

Scene I. [Another part of the island.]

*Enter Alonso, Sebastian, Antonio, Gonzalo, Adrian,
Francisco, and others.*

Gon. Beseech you, sir, be merry. You have cause
(So have we all) of joy; for our escape
Is much beyond our loss. Our hint of woe
Is common. Every day some sailor's wife,
The master of some merchant, and the merchant,   5
Have just our theme of woe; but for the miracle,
I mean our preservation, few in millions
Can speak like us. Then wisely, good sir, weigh
Our sorrow with our comfort.

Alon.   Prithee peace.   10

Seb. He receives comfort like cold porridge.

Ant. The visitor will not give him o'er so.

Seb. Look, he's winding up the watch of his wit;
by-and-by it will strike.

Gon. Sir—   15

Seb. One. Tell.

Gon. When every grief is entertained that's offered,

26

23. **wiselier:** Sebastian did not expect Gonzalo to grasp his double meaning.

34. **The wager:** i.e., what is the prize?

35. **laughter:** i.e., nothing except a good laugh.

36. **A match:** agreed!

44-5. **subtle, tender, and delicate temperance:** moderate climate.

46. **Temperance:** in use as a feminine name; also one of the virtues frequently pictured in personified form as a woman.

47-8. **delivered:** reported.

Temperance.
From Jost Amman, *Stam und Wapenbuch* (1579).

Comes to the entertainer—

Seb. A dollar. 20

Gon. Dolor comes to him, indeed. You have spoken
truer than you purposed.

Seb. You have taken it wiselier than I meant you
should.

Gon. Therefore, my lord— 25

Ant. Fie, what a spendthrift is he of his tongue!

Alon. I prithee spare.

Gon. Well, I have done. But yet—

Seb. He will be talking.

Ant. Which, of he or Adrian, for a good wager, 30
first begins to crow?

Seb. The old cock.

Ant. The cock'rel.

Seb. Done! The wager?

Ant. A laughter. 35

Seb. A match!

Adr. Though this island seem to be desert—

Ant. Ha, ha, ha!

Seb. So, you're paid.

Adr. Uninhabitable and almost inaccessible— 40

Seb. Yet—

Adr. Yet—

Ant. He could not miss't.

Adr. It must needs be of subtle, tender, and delicate temperance. 45

Ant. Temperance was a delicate wench.

Seb. Ay, and a subtle, as he most learnedly delivered.

Adr. The air breathes upon us here most sweetly.

55. **lusty:** plentiful.

61. **rarity:** i.e., most unusual feature.

63. **vouched:** avouched. Sebastian refers to travelers' tales of curious sights.

70. **pocket up:** accept without protest. The phrase was usually used with reference to an insult or false accusation.

79. **widow Dido:** the widowed Queen of Carthage (now Tunis), who fell in love with Aeneas.

Seb. As if it had lungs, and rotten ones. 50

Ant. Or as 'twere perfumed by a fen.

Gon. Here is everything advantageous to life.

Ant. True; save means to live.

Seb. Of that there's none, or little.

Gon. How lush and lusty the grass looks! how 55
green!

Ant. The ground indeed is tawny.

Seb. With an eye of green in't.

Ant. He misses not much.

Seb. No; he doth but mistake the truth totally. 60

Gon. But the rarity of it is—which is indeed almost
beyond credit—

Seb. As many vouched rarities are.

Gon. That our garments, being, as they were,
drenched in the sea, hold, notwithstanding, their 65
freshness and gloss, being rather new-dyed than
stained with salt water.

Ant. If but one of his pockets could speak, would
it not say he lies?

Seb. Ay, or very falsely pocket up his report. 70

Gon. Methinks our garments are now as fresh as
when we put them on first in Afric, at the marriage
of the King's fair daughter Claribel to the King of
Tunis.

Seb. 'Twas a sweet marriage, and we prosper well 75
in our return.

Adr. Tunis was never graced before with such a
paragon to their queen.

Gon. Not since widow Dido's time.

89. **His word is more than the miraculous harp:** i.e., if he can re-create ruined Carthage in modern Tunis, he has more amazing powers than Amphion, the legendary bard who raised the walls of Thebes by playing on his harp.

103. **Bate:** leave out of account. Antonio sarcastically suggests that Gonzalo should except the widow Dido when he calls Claribel the rarest queen that ever came to Tunis.

105. **doublet:** jacket.

106. **in a sort:** more or less.

109-10. **against/The stomach of my sense:** so as to wound my sensibilities.

Amphion raising the walls of Thebes.
From Philostratus, *Les images ou tableaux de platte peinture* (1629).

Ant. Widow? A pox o' that! How came that "wid- 80
ow" in? Widow Dido!

Seb. What if he had said "widower Aeneas" too?
Good Lord, how you take it!

Adr. "Widow Dido," said you? You make me study
of that. She was of Carthage, not of Tunis. 85

Gon. This Tunis, sir, was Carthage.

Adr. Carthage?

Gon. I assure you, Carthage.

Ant. His word is more than the miraculous harp.

Seb. He hath raised the wall, and houses too. 90

Ant. What impossible matter will he make easy
next?

Seb. I think he will carry this island home in his
pocket and give it his son for an apple.

Ant. And, sowing the kernels of it in the sea, bring 95
forth more islands.

Gon. Ay!

Ant. Why, in good time!

Gon. Sir, we were talking that our garments seem
now as fresh as when we were at Tunis at the mar- 100
riage of your daughter, who is now Queen.

Ant. And the rarest that e'er came there.

Seb. Bate, I beseech you, widow Dido.

Ant. O, widow Dido? Ay, widow Dido!

Gon. Is not, sir, my doublet as fresh as the first 105
day I wore it? I mean, in a sort.

Ant. That "sort" was well fished for.

Gon. When I wore it at your daughter's marriage.

Alon. You cram these words into mine ears against
The stomach of my sense. Would I had never 110

112. **in my rate:** so far as I am concerned.

137. **Weighed:** balanced; swayed; **loathness:** reluctance.

138. **Which end o' the beam should bow:** i.e., which should weigh the heaviest.

Married my daughter there! for, coming thence,
My son is lost; and, in my rate, she too,
Who is so far from Italy removed
I ne'er again shall see her. O thou mine heir
Of Naples and of Milan, what strange fish   115
Hath made his meal on thee?

   Fran.   Sir, he may live.
I saw him beat the surges under him
And ride upon their backs. He trod the water,
Whose enmity he flung aside, and breasted   120
The surge most swol'n that met him. His bold head
'Bove the contentious waves he kept, and oared
Himself with his good arms in lusty stroke
To the shore, that o'er his wave-worn basis bowed,
As stooping to relieve him. I not doubt   125
He came alive to land.

   Alon.   No, no, he's gone.

   Seb. Sir, you may thank yourself for this great loss,
That would not bless our Europe with your daughter,
But rather lose her to an African,   130
Where she, at least, is banished from your eye
Who hath cause to wet the grief on't.

   Alon.   Prithee peace.

   Seb. You were kneeled to and importuned other-
     wise   135
By all of us; and the fair soul herself
Weighed, between loathness and obedience, at
Which end o' the beam should bow. We have lost
     your son,
I fear, forever. Milan and Naples have   140

141. **Mo:** more.

147. **time:** suitable time. When the King's loss is so fresh, it is inappropriate to suggest that he has only himself to blame.

150. **chirurgeonly:** like a professional surgeon.

152. **cloudy:** downcast.

157. **docks . . . mallows:** two common wild plants.

160. **by contraries:** contrarily to what is generally done.

163. **Letters:** literary production and learning.

165. **Bourn:** boundary; **tilth:** tillage of the soil; agriculture.

Mo widows in them of this business' making
Than we bring men to comfort them.
The fault's your own.

  Alon.   So is the dear'st o' the loss.

  Gon. My Lord Sebastian,   145
The truth you speak doth lack some gentleness,
And time to speak it in. You rub the sore
When you should bring the plaster.

  Seb.   Very well.

  Ant. And most chirurgeonly.   150

  Gon. It is foul weather in us all, good sir,
When you are cloudy.

  Seb.   Foul weather?

  Ant.   Very foul.

  Gon. Had I plantation of this isle, my lord—   155

  Ant. He'd sow't with nettle seed.

  Seb.   Or docks, or mallows.

  Gon. And were the king on't, what would I do?

  Seb. 'Scape being drunk, for want of wine.

  Gon. I' the commonwealth I would by contraries 160
Execute all things; for no kind of traffic
Would I admit; no name of magistrate;
Letters should not be known; riches, poverty,
And use of service, none; contract, succession,
Bourn, bound of land, tilth, vineyard, none;   165
No use of metal, corn, or wine, or oil;
No occupation; all men idle, all;
And women too, but innocent and pure;
No sovereignty.

  Seb.   Yet he would be king on't.   170

175. **engine:** military machine.

177. **it:** its; **foison:** plenty.

182. **the golden age:** in classical belief, an age when man lived without labor, crime, or pain, as Adam lived in Eden before the Fall.

183. **Save:** long live.

189. **minister occasion:** give occasion for mirth.

190. **sensible:** responsive.

197. **flatlong:** that is, on the flat instead of the point.

198. **brave metal:** fine quality.

Ant. The latter end of his commonwealth forgets
the beginning.

Gon. All things in common nature should produce
Without sweat or endeavor. Treason, felony,
Sword, pike, knife, gun, or need of any engine　　175
Would I not have; but nature should bring forth,
Of it own kind, all foison, all abundance,
To feed my innocent people.

Seb. No marrying 'mong his subjects?

Ant. None, man! All idle—whores and knaves.　　180

Gon. I would with such perfection govern, sir,
T'excel the golden age.

Seb.　　　　　　　Save his Majesty!

Ant. Long live Gonzalo!

Gon.　　　　　　　And—do you mark me, sir?　　185

Alon. Prithee no more. Thou dost talk nothing to
me.

Gon. I do well believe your Highness; and did it to
minister occasion to these gentlemen, who are of
such sensible and nimble lungs that they always use　190
to laugh at nothing.

Ant. 'Twas you we laughed at.

Gon. Who in this kind of merry fooling am nothing
to you. So you may continue, and laugh at nothing still.　　195

Ant. What a blow was there given!

Seb. An it had not fall'n flatlong.

Gon. You are gentlemen of brave metal. You would
lift the moon out of her sphere if she would continue
in it five weeks without changing.　　200

201. **a-batfowling:** a method of fowling at night. The birds were aroused from their roosts, confused by lights, and beaten down with bats. Sebastian would use the moon for the necessary light.

203-4. **adventure my discretion so weakly:** risk my reputation as a sensible man for so little reason.

211. **omit the heavy offer of it:** let pass the opportunity to sleep offered by your drowsiness.

219. **quality:** nature.

224. **consent:** agreement.

Enter Ariel, [invisible], playing solemn music.

Seb. We would so, and then go a-batfowling.
Ant. Nay, good my lord, be not angry.
Gon. No, I warrant you. I will not adventure my
discretion so weakly. Will you laugh me asleep, for I
am very heavy? 205
Ant. Go sleep, and hear us.
[*All sleep except Alonso, Sebastian, and Antonio.*]
Alon. What, all so soon asleep? I wish mine eyes
Would, with themselves, shut up my thoughts. I find
They are inclined to do so.
Seb.   Please you, sir 210
Do not omit the heavy offer of it.
It seldom visits sorrow; when it doth,
It is a comforter.
Ant.   We two, my lord,
Will guard your person while you take your rest, 215
And watch your safety.
Alon.   Thank you. Wondrous heavy.
                              [*Alonso sleeps. Exit Ariel.*]
Seb. What a strange drowsiness possesses them!
Ant. It is the quality o' the climate.
Seb.   Why 220
Doth it not then our eyelids sink? I find not
Myself disposed to sleep.
Ant.   Nor I. My spirits are nimble.
They fell together all, as by consent.
They dropped as by a thunderstroke. What might, 225
Worthy Sebastian—O, what might?—No more!
And yet methinks I see it in thy face,

228. **The occasion speaks thee:** opportunity bespeaks (names) thee.

240. **winkst:** close your eyes.

242. **distinctly:** intelligibly; i.e., his snores are words.

245. **if heed me:** if you heed me.

246. **Trebles thee o'er:** will make you three times greater than you are.

247. **standing water:** i.e., a receptive listener.

252. **cherish:** foster.

253-54. **in stripping it,/You more invest it:** in belittling it, you make it greater.

What thou shouldst be. The occasion speaks thee, and
My strong imagination sees a crown
Dropping upon thy head.   230

  Seb.   What? Art thou waking?

  Ant. Do you not hear me speak?

  Seb.   I do; and surely
It is a sleepy language, and thou speakst
Out of thy sleep. What is it thou didst say?   23~
This is a strange repose, to be asleep
With eyes wide open; standing, speaking, moving—
And yet so fast asleep.

  Ant.   Noble Sebastian,
Thou letst thy fortune sleep—die, rather; winkst   240
Whiles thou art waking.

  Seb.   Thou dost snore distinctly;
There's meaning in thy snores.

  Ant. I am more serious than my custom. You
Must be so too, if heed me; which to do   245
Trebles thee o'er.

  Seb.   Well, I am standing water.

  Ant. I'll teach you how to flow.

  Seb.   Do so. To ebb
Hereditary sloth instructs me.   250

  Ant.   O,
If you but knew how you the purpose cherish
Whiles thus you mock it! how, in stripping it,
You more invest it! Ebbing men indeed
(Most often) do so near the bottom run   255
By their own fear or sloth.

  Seb.   Prithee say on.
The setting of thine eye and cheek proclaim

259. **matter:** matter of importance.

260. **throes thee much:** causes you great effort.

262. **this lord of weak remembrance:** Francisco, whose story of Ferdinand's escape from death is disbelieved by Antonio.

263-64. **of as little memory/When he is earthed:** as little remembered when he is buried.

265-66. **only/Professes to persuade:** that is, persuasion is his only occupation.

274. **wink:** i.e., the slightest bit.

275. **doubts discovery there:** doubts what he sees revealed there; cannot believe his good fortune.

282. **beyond man's life:** farther than one could travel in the span of human life.

283. **note:** information; **post:** messenger (riding posthaste).

285. **from whom:** i.e., traveling from whom. The ship was returning from her wedding as indicated in ll. 110-12.

286. **cast:** cast up by the sea.

288. **what's past is prologue:** i.e., Claribel's marriage so far from Naples and the wreck that cost Ferdinand his life are preliminaries.

289. **In yours and my discharge:** due to be performed by you and me.

A matter from thee; and a birth, indeed,
Which throes thee much to yield.   260
    Ant.   Thus, sir:
Although this lord of weak remembrance, this
Who shall be of as little memory
When he is earthed, hath here almost persuaded
(For he's a spirit of persuasion, only   265
Professes to persuade) the King his son's alive,
'Tis as impossible that he's undrowned
As he that sleeps here swims.
    Seb.   I have no hope
That he's undrowned.   270
    Ant.   O, out of that no hope
What great hope have you! No hope that way is
Another way so high a hope that even
Ambition cannot pierce a wink beyond,
But doubts discovery there. Will you grant with me   275
That Ferdinand is drowned?
    Seb.   He's gone.
    Ant.   Then tell me,
Who's the next heir of Naples?
    Seb.   Claribel.   280
    Ant. She that is Queen of Tunis; she that dwells
Ten leagues beyond man's life; she that from Naples
Can have no note, unless the sun were post—
The man i' the moon's too slow—till newborn chins
Be rough and razorable; she that from whom   285
We all were sea-swallowed, though some cast again,
And, by that destiny, to perform an act
Whereof what's past is prologue, what to come,
In yours and my discharge.

296. **Measure us:** tread the distance that we (the cubits) measure.

298. **them:** their sleeping companions.

302-3. **make/A chough of as deep chat:** train a jackdaw to talk as profoundly.

307-8. **how does your content/Tender your own good fortune:** how does your good fortune content you?

313. **feater:** more neatly or aptly.

316. **kibe:** chilblain or chafed spot on the heel.

317. **put me to my slipper:** cause me to wear slippers for comfort.

319. **candied:** frozen.

Seb.   What stuff is this? How say you? 290
'Tis true my brother's daughter's Queen of Tunis;
So is she heir of Naples; 'twixt which regions
There is some space.
    Ant.   A space whose ev'ry cubit
Seems to cry out "How shall that Claribel   295
Measure us back to Naples? Keep in Tunis,
And let Sebastian wake!" Say this were death
That now hath seized them, why, they were no worse
Than now they are. There be that can rule Naples
As well as he that sleeps; lords that can prate   300
As amply and unnecessarily
As this Gonzalo. I myself could make
A chough of as deep chat. O, that you bore
The mind that I do! What a sleep were this
For your advancement! Do you understand me?   305
    Seb. Methinks I do.
    Ant.   And how does your content
Tender your own good fortune?
    Seb.   I remember
You did supplant your brother Prospero.   310
    Ant.   True.
And look how well my garments sit upon me,
Much feater than before! My brother's servants
Were then my fellows; now they are my men.
    Seb. But, for your conscience—   315
    Ant. Ay, sir! Where lies that? If 'twere a kibe,
'Twould put me to my slipper; but I feel not
This deity in my bosom. Twenty consciences
That stand 'twixt me and Milan, candied be they
And melt, ere they molest! Here lies your brother,   320

325. **wink:** closed eye.

326-27. **ancient morsel:** old scrap of manhood; i.e., Gonzalo; **who/Should not:** so that he shall not.

328. **suggestion:** evil suggestion; temptation.

329. **tell the clock:** i.e., announce that the time has come. Their reaction will be "The sooner the better."

338. **fall:** drop.

No better than the earth he lies upon
If he were that which now he's like—that's dead;
Whom I with this obedient steel (three inches of it)
Can lay to bed forever; whiles you, doing thus,
To the perpetual wink for aye might put   325
This ancient morsel, this Sir Prudence, who
Should not upbraid our course. For all the rest,
They'll take suggestion as a cat laps milk;
They'll tell the clock to any business that
We say befits the hour.   330
  Seb.   Thy case, dear friend,
Shall be my precedent. As thou gotst Milan,
I'll come by Naples. Draw thy sword. One stroke
Shall free thee from the tribute which thou payest,
And I the King shall love thee.   335
  Ant.   Draw together;
And when I rear my hand, do you the like,
To fall it on Gonzalo.   [*They draw.*]
  Seb.   O, but one word!
          [*They converse apart.*]

Enter Ariel, [invisible], with music and song.

  Ariel. My master through his art foresees the   340
    danger
That you, his friend, are in, and sends me forth
(For else his project dies) to keep them living.
          Sings in Gonzalo's ear.

          While you here do snoring lie,
          Open-eyed conspiracy   345
            His time doth take.

357. **Even:** just.
369. **verily:** truth.

                 If of life you keep a care,
                 Shake off slumber and beware.
                    Awake, awake!

Ant. Then let us both be sudden.   350
Gon. [*Wakes*] Now good angels preserve the King!
Alon. [*Wakes*] Why, how now? Ho, awake! Why
     are you drawn?
Wherefore this ghastly looking?
Gon.   What's the matter?   355
Seb. Whiles we stood here securing your repose,
Even now, we heard a hollow burst of bellowing
Like bulls, or rather lions. Did't not wake you?
It struck mine ear most terribly.
Alon.   I heard nothing.   360
Ant. O, 'twas a din to fright a monster's ear,
To make an earthquake! Sure it was the roar
Of a whole herd of lions.
Alon.   Heard you this, Gonzalo?
Gon. Upon mine honor, sir, I heard a humming,   365
And that a strange one too, which did awake me.
I shaked you, sir, and cried. As mine eyes opened,
I saw their weapons drawn. There was a noise;
That's verily. 'Tis best we stand upon our guard,
Or that we quit this place. Let's draw our weapons.   370
Alon. Lead off this ground, and let's make further
     search
For my poor son.
Gon.   Heavens keep him from these beasts!
For he is sure i' the island.   375
Alon.   Lead away.

II. ii. Caliban, gathering wood for Prospero, lies down to escape the notice of Trinculo, whom he takes to be one of Prospero's spirits sent to torment him. Trinculo, fearing another storm, crawls under Caliban's cloak, though he is repelled by the monster's smell and grotesque appearance. Another castaway, Stephano, enters singing tipsily. Spying the strange combination of Trinculo and Caliban, he thinks he has found a rare monster. He gives each some of his wine and he and Trinculo eventually recognize each other. Caliban is so affected by his first taste of alcohol that he thinks Stephano is a god and swears to serve him. Stephano assumes that they own the island, since the rest of the ship's party have apparently perished. Caliban sings an exultant song of liberation from Prospero's service as he leads his new master to see the wonders of the isle.

3. **By inchmeal:** inch by inch.
5. **urchin-shows:** imp appearances; see I. ii. 400.
6. **firebrand:** will-o'-the-wisp.
9. **mow:** grimace.

Ariel. Prospero my lord shall know what I have
 done.
So, King, go safely on to seek thy son.

Exeunt.

Scene II. [Another part of the island.]

*Enter Caliban with a burden of wood. A noise of
thunder heard.*

Cal. All the infections that the sun sucks up
From bogs, fens, flats, on Prosper fall and make him
By inchmeal a disease! His spirits hear me,
And yet I needs must curse. But they'll nor pinch,
Fright me with urchin-shows, pitch me i' the mire,   5
Nor lead me, like a firebrand, in the dark
Out of my way, unless he bid 'em; but
For every trifle are they set upon me;
Sometime like apes that mow and chatter at me,
And after bite me; then like hedgehogs which   10
Lie tumbling in my barefoot way and mount
Their pricks at my footfall; sometime am I
All wound with adders, who with cloven tongues
Do hiss me into madness.

Enter Trinculo.

Lo, now, lo!   15
Here comes a spirit of his, and to torment me
For bringing wood in slowly. I'll fall flat;

18. **mind:** notice.

22. **bombard:** leather drinking vessel.

24-5. **cannot choose but:** i.e., cannot fail to.

28-31. **poor John:** dried and salted fish; **Were . . . silver:** a reference to the English fondness for freaks and monsters in side shows; **make a man:** i.e., make a man rich.

33. **doit:** a coin of little value.

35. **o' my troth:** on my faith.

39. **gaberdine:** cloak.

Perchance he will not mind me.   [*Lies down.*]

   Trin. Here's neither bush nor shrub to bear off any
weather at all, and another storm brewing. I hear it   20
sing i' the wind. Yond same black cloud, yond huge
one, looks like a foul bombard that would shed his
liquor. If it should thunder as it did before, I know
not where to hide my head. Yond same cloud cannot
choose but fall by pailfuls. What have we here? a   25
man or a fish? dead or alive? A fish: he smells like a
fish; a very ancient and fishlike smell; a kind of, not
of the newest, poor John. A strange fish! Were I in
England now, as once I was, and had but this fish
painted, not a holiday fool there but would give a   30
piece of silver. There would this monster make a man.
Any strange beast there makes a man. When they
will not give a doit to relieve a lame beggar, they
will lay out ten to see a dead Indian. Legged like a
man! and his fins like arms! Warm, o' my troth! I do   35
now let loose my opinion, hold it no longer: this is no
fish, but an islander, that hath lately suffered by a
thunderbolt. [*Thunder.*] Alas, the storm is come
again! My best way is to creep under his gaberdine.
There is no other shelter hereabout. Misery acquaints   40
a man with strange bedfellows. I will here shroud till
the dregs of the storm be past.

         [*Creeps under Caliban's garment.*]

Enter Stephano, singing; [a bottle in his hand].

  Ste.   I shall no more to sea, to sea;
            Here shall I die ashore.

45. **scurvy:** contemptible.

49. **Mall:** a nickname for Mary.

60. **upon's:** upon us; **Inde:** India, or the Indies.

62. **your four legs:** i.e., all four-legged creatures; **proper:** manly.

70. **recover:** cure.

72. **neat's:** cow's.

This is a very scurvy tune to sing at a man's funeral.   45
Well, here's my comfort.   *Drinks.*

> The master, the swabber, the boatswain, and I,
>   The gunner, and his mate,
> Loved Mall, Meg, and Marian, and Margery,
>   But none of us cared for Kate.   50
>   For she had a tongue with a tang,
>   Would cry to a sailor "Go hang!"
> She loved not the savor of tar nor of pitch;
> Yet a tailor might scratch her where'er she did
>   itch.   55
>   Then to sea, boys, and let her go hang!

This is a scurvy tune too; but here's my comfort.
                                            Drinks.

Cal. Do not torment me! O!

Ste. What's the matter? Have we devils here? Do
you put tricks upon's with savages and men of Inde,   60
ha? I have not 'scaped drowning to be afeard now of
your four legs; for it hath been said, "As proper a
man as ever went on four legs cannot make him give
ground"; and it shall be said so again, while Stephano
breathes at nostrils.   65

Cal. The spirit torments me. O!

Ste. This is some monster of the isle, with four
legs, who hath got, as I take it, an ague. Where the
devil should he learn our language? I will give him
some relief, if it be but for that. If I can recover him,   70
and keep him tame, and get to Naples with him, he's
a present for any emperor that ever trod on neat's
leather.

76-7. **after the wisest:** i.e., in the most sensible manner.

79-81. **I will not take too much:** i.e., no price I can ask will be too much; **he shall pay for him that hath him, and that soundly:** whoever buys him shall pay handsomely for him.

85. **Come on your ways:** come on (open your mouth).

86. **cat:** referring to the proverb "Good ale (or liquor) will make a cat speak."

89. **chaps:** jaws.

92-3. **Four legs and two voices:** Trinculo has crept under Caliban's robe so that his feet protrude by Caliban's head and vice versa. The tipsy Stephano thinks he is dealing with a creature that has four legs and two heads; **delicate monster:** i.e., a monster of the choicest sort; a real rarity.

97. **Amen:** "Well done," as Caliban drinks lustily.

100-1. **I have no long spoon:** an allusion to the proverb "He should have a long spoon that sups with the Devil."

Cal. Do not torment me prithee! I'll bring my wood home faster. 75

Ste. He's in his fit now and does not talk after the wisest. He shall taste of my bottle. If he have never drunk wine afore, it will go near to remove his fit. If I can recover him and keep him tame, I will not take too much for him; he shall pay for him that hath 80 him, and that soundly.

Cal. Thou dost me yet but little hurt. Thou wilt anon; I know it by thy trembling. Now Prosper works upon thee.

Ste. Come on your ways. Open your mouth. Here 85 is that which will give language to you, cat. Open your mouth. This will shake your shaking, I can tell you, and that soundly. [*Gives Caliban drink.*] You cannot tell who's your friend. Open your chaps again.

Trin. I should know that voice. It should be—but 90 he is drowned; and these are devils. O, defend me!

Ste. Four legs and two voices—a most delicate monster! His forward voice now is to speak well of his friend; his backward voice is to utter foul speeches and to detract. If all the wine in my bottle will re- 95 cover him, I will help his ague. Come! [*Gives drink.*] Amen! I will pour some in thy other mouth.

Trin. Stephano!

Ste. Doth thy other mouth call me? Mercy, mercy! This is a devil, and no monster. I will leave him; I 100 have no long spoon.

Trin. Stephano! If thou beest Stephano, touch me and speak to me; for I am Trinculo—be not afeard— thy good friend Trinculo.

108-9. **siege:** excrement; **mooncalf:** freak.
117. **constant:** steady.
118. **an if:** if.
123. **butt of sack:** barrel of sherry wine.
133-34. **like a goose:** i.e., stupid.

Ste. If thou beest Trinculo, come forth. I'll pull 105
thee by the lesser legs. If any be Trinculo's legs, these
are they. [*Pulls him out.*] Thou art very Trinculo indeed! How camest thou to be the siege of this mooncalf? Can he vent Trinculos?

Trin. I took him to be killed with a thunderstroke. 110
But art thou not drowned, Stephano? I hope now
thou art not drowned. Is the storm overblown? I hid
me under the dead mooncalf's gaberdine for fear of
the storm. And art thou living, Stephano? O Stephano, two Neapolitans 'scaped? 115

Ste. Prithee do not turn me about. My stomach is
not constant.

Cal. [*Aside*] These be fine things, an if they be not
sprites. That's a brave god and bears celestial liquor.
I will kneel to him. 120

Ste. How didst thou 'scape? How camest thou
hither? Swear by this bottle how thou camest hither.
I escaped upon a butt of sack which the sailors
heaved o'erboard, by this bottle, which I made of the
bark of a tree with mine own hands since I was cast 125
ashore.

Cal. I'll swear upon that bottle to be thy true subject, for the liquor is not earthly.

Ste. Here! Swear then how thou escapedst.

Trin. Swum ashore, man, like a duck. I can swim 130
like a duck, I'll be sworn.

Ste. Here, kiss the book. [*Gives him drink.*] Though
thou canst swim like a duck, thou art made like a
goose.

141. **when time was:** at one time.

143-44. **thy dog, and thy bush:** the accompaniments of a man in an old tale, who was placed on the moon as a punishment and became the Man in the Moon.

147. **shallow:** empty-headed; witless.

150. **Well drawn:** Caliban has just taken a deep draught of the wine.

Trin. O Stephano, hast any more of this? 135

Ste. The whole butt, man. My cellar is in a rock by the seaside, where my wine is hid. How now, mooncalf? How does thine ague?

Cal. Hast thou not dropped from heaven?

Ste. Out o' the moon, I do assure thee. I was the 140
Man i' the Moon when time was.

Cal. I have seen thee in her, and I do adore thee. My mistress showed me thee, and thy dog, and thy bush.

Ste. Come, swear to that; kiss the book. I will fur- 145
nish it anon with new contents. Swear.

[*Caliban drinks.*]

Trin. By this good light, this is a very shallow monster! I afeard of him? A very weak monster! The Man i' the Moon? A most poor credulous monster! Well drawn, monster, in good sooth. 150

Cal. I'll show thee every fertile inch o' the island; and I will kiss thy foot. I prithee be my god.

Trin. By this light, a most perfidious and drunken monster! When's god's asleep he'll rob his bottle.

Cal. I'll kiss thy foot. I'll swear myself thy subject. 155

Ste. Come on then. Down, and swear!

Trin. I shall laugh myself to death at this puppy-headed monster. A most scurvy monster! I could find in my heart to beat him—

Ste. Come, kiss. 160

Trin. But that the poor monster's in drink. An abominable monster!

Cal. I'll show thee the best springs; I'll pluck thee berries;

171. **crabs:** crab apples.

172. **pignuts:** edible tubers.

174. **marmoset:** i.e., probably some variety of monkey rather than the true **marmoset.**

176. **scamels:** an unexplained word which occurs nowhere else. Probably this is a misprint for "sea mews," a variety of sea bird.

186. **trenchering:** a trencher is a wooden platter. Caliban probably means to say "trencher scraping."

189. **highday:** heyday.

I'll fish for thee, and get thee wood enough.   165
A plague upon the tyrant that I serve!
I'll bear him no more sticks, but follow thee,
Thou wondrous man.

Trin. A most ridiculous monster, to make a wonder of a poor drunkard!   170

Cal. I prithee let me bring thee where crabs grow;
And I with my long nails will dig thee pignuts,
Show thee a jay's nest, and instruct thee how
To snare the nimble marmoset; I'll bring thee
To clust'ring filberts, and sometimes I'll get thee   175
Young scamels from the rock. Wilt thou go with me?

Ste. I prithee now lead the way without any more
talking. Trinculo, the King and all our company else
being drowned, we will inherit here. Here, bear my
bottle. Fellow Trinculo, we'll fill him by-and-by again.   180
Caliban sings drunkenly.

Cal. Farewell, master; farewell, farewell!
Trin. A howling monster! a drunken monster!

Cal. No more dams I'll make for fish,
　　　Nor fetch in firing
　　　At requiring,   185
　Nor scrape trenchering, nor wash dish.
　　'Ban, 'Ban, Ca—Caliban
　　Has a new master. Get a new man.

Freedom, highday! highday, freedom! freedom, highday, freedom!   190
Ste. O brave monster! lead the way.

Exeunt.

THE TEMPEST

ACT III

III. i. Prospero has set Ferdinand to carrying wood to test his love for his daughter. Miranda is distressed at Ferdinand's labor and offers to do the work for him. They confess their love for each other, and Prospero, who has been watching unseen, is pleased at the progress of his plans.

▪▪▪▪▪▪▪▪▪▪▪▪▪▪▪▪▪▪▪▪▪▪▪▪▪▪▪▪

1-3. **some sports are painful, and their labor/ Delight in them sets off:** i.e., some sports are physically taxing, but the pleasure they give us cancels the labor.

4. **most poor:** the poorest.

7. **quickens:** enlivens.

10. **composed of:** i.e., wholly made up of.

12. **Upon a sore injunction:** in accordance with a stern command (with the implication of painful consequences if he fails to carry out the command).

15. **forget:** that is, forget myself in my thoughts and slack my work.

17. **Most busy least when I do it:** my busiest moment seems my least busy when pleasant thoughts of Miranda cause me to forget that I am working.

ACT III

Scene I. [Before Prospero's cell.]

Enter Ferdinand, bearing a log.

Fer. There be some sports are painful, and their labor
Delight in them sets off; some kinds of baseness
Are nobly undergone, and most poor matters
Point to rich ends. This my mean task   5
Would be as heavy to me as odious, but
The mistress which I serve quickens what's dead
And makes my labors pleasures. O, she is
Ten times more gentle than her father's crabbed;
And he's composed of harshness! I must remove   10
Some thousands of these logs and pile them up,
Upon a sore injunction. My sweet mistress
Weeps when she sees me work, and says such baseness
Had never like executor. I forget;   15
But these sweet thoughts do even refresh my labors.
Most busy least when I do it.

24. **safe:** no danger.

Enter Miranda; and Prospero [behind, unseen].

Mir.   Alas, now pray you
Work not so hard! I would the lightning had
Burnt up those logs that you are enjoined to pile!   20
Pray set it down and rest you. When this burns,
'Twill weep for having wearied you. My father
Is hard at study; pray now rest yourself;
He's safe for these three hours.
    Fer.   O most dear mistress,   25
The sun will set before I shall discharge
What I must strive to do.
    Mir.   If you'll sit down,
I'll bear your logs the while. Pray give me that.
I'll carry it to the pile.   30
    Fer.   No, precious creature.
I had rather crack my sinews, break my back,
Than you should such dishonor undergo
While I sit lazy by.
    Mir.   It would become me   35
As well as it does you; and I should do it
With much more ease; for my good will is to it,
And yours it is against.
    Pros. [*Aside*]   Poor worm, thou art infected!
This visitation shows it.   40
    Mir.   You look wearily.
    Fer. No, noble mistress. 'Tis fresh morning with me
When you are by at night. I do beseech you,
Chiefly that I might set it in my prayers,
What is your name?   45

47. **hest:** command; see I. ii. 332.

48. **Admired:** admirable.

51. **best regard:** closest attention.

56. **owed:** owned.

57. **put it to the foil:** foiled it; destroyed its effect.

64. **abroad:** in the world at large.

65. **skill-less of:** uninformed about.

72. **condition:** rank.

76. **flesh fly:** a fly that lays its eggs in flesh; **blow:** i.e., swell, by a deposit of its eggs.

Mir.   Miranda. O my father,
I have broke your hest to say so!
    Fer.   Admired Miranda!
Indeed the top of admiration, worth
What's dearest to the world! Full many a lady   50
I have eyed with best regard, and many a time
The harmony of their tongues hath into bondage
Brought my too diligent ear; for several virtues
Have I liked several women; never any
With so full soul but some defect in her   55
Did quarrel with the noblest grace she owed,
And put it to the foil; but you, O you,
So perfect and so peerless, are created
Of every creature's best!
    Mir.   I do not know   60
One of my sex; no woman's face remember,
Save, from my glass, mine own; nor have I seen
More that I may call men than you, good friend,
And my dear father. How features are abroad
I am skill-less of; but, by my modesty   65
(The jewel in my dower), I would not wish
Any companion in the world but you;
Nor can imagination form a shape,
Besides yourself, to like of. But I prattle
Something too wildly, and my father's precepts   70
I therein do forget.
    Fer.   I am, in my condition,
A prince, Miranda; I do think, a king
(I would not so!), and would no more endure
This wooden slavery than to suffer   75
The flesh fly blow my mouth. Hear my soul speak!

83. **event:** outcome; see I. ii. 139.

90. **Fair encounter:** equal match.

96. **want:** lack.

98. **Hence, bashful cunning:** away with round-about hints prompted by modesty.

101. **fellow:** mate.

104. **mistress:** ruler of my heart.

The very instant that I saw you, did
My heart fly to your service, there resides,
To make me slave to it; and for your sake
Am I this patient log-man.   80

    Mir.   Do you love me?

    Fer. O heaven, O earth, bear witness to this sound,
And crown what I profess with kind event
If I speak true! if hollowly, invert
What best is boded me to mischief! I,   85
Beyond all limit of what else i' the world,
Do love, prize, honor you.

    Mir.   I am a fool
To weep at what I am glad of.

    Pros. [*Aside*]   Fair encounter   90
Of two most rare affections! Heavens rain grace
On that which breeds between 'em!

    Fer.   Wherefore weep you?

    Mir. At mine unworthiness, that dare not offer
What I desire to give, and much less take   95
What I shall die to want. But this is trifling;
And all the more it seeks to hide itself,
The bigger bulk it shows. Hence, bashful cunning!
And prompt me plain and holy innocence!
I am your wife, if you will marry me;   100
If not, I'll die your maid. To be your fellow
You may deny me; but I'll be your servant,
Whether you will or no.

    Fer.   My mistress, dearest!
And I thus humble ever.   105

    Mir.   My husband then?

    Fer. Ay, with a heart as willing

114. surprised: Prospero refers to the fact that he has planned this match, while Ferdinand and Miranda had no foreknowledge that they would meet and fall in love.

▬▬▬▬▬▬▬▬▬▬▬▬▬▬▬▬▬▬▬▬

III. ii. Caliban, Trinculo, and Stephano have been drinking wine freely. Caliban urges his "god" to free him by murdering Prospero; then the island will belong to Stephano, who can have Miranda as his woman. Stephano is convinced, but invisible Ariel has overheard the plot and, playing music, lures them away.

▬▬▬▬▬▬▬▬▬▬▬▬▬▬▬

1. **Tell not me:** don't talk to me of saving our wine.

2-3. **bear up and board 'em:** a naval order to engage with a hostile vessel; i.e., drink like a man.

9. **almost set:** glazed from the wine's effect.

As bondage e'er of freedom. Here's my hand.

  Mir. And mine, with my heart in't; and now farewell 110
Till half an hour hence.

  Fer.   A thousand thousand!

        Exeunt [Ferdinand and Miranda severally].

  Pros. So glad of this as they I cannot be,
Who are surprised withal; but my rejoicing
At nothing can be more. I'll to my book; 115
For yet ere suppertime must I perform
Much business appertaining.

                          Exit.

Scene II. [Another part of the island.]

Enter Caliban, Stephano, and Trinculo.

  Ste. Tell not me! When the butt is out, we will drink water; not a drop before. Therefore bear up and board 'em! Servant monster, drink to me.

  Trin. Servant monster? The folly of this island! They say there's but five upon this isle. We are three 5
of them. If the other two be brained like us, the state totters.

  Ste. Drink, servant monster, when I bid thee. Thy eyes are almost set in thy head.

  Trin. Where should they be set else? He were a 10
brave monster indeed if they were set in his tail.

16. **standard:** standard-bearer.

17. **list:** please; **standard:** i.e., the wine has made him barely able to stand up.

25-6. **in case:** in condition (made valiant by drink); **deboshed:** debauched.

33. **natural:** idiot, with a pun. A monster is not **natural.**

41. **Marry:** "by the Virgin Mary"; indeed.

Ste. My man-monster hath drowned his tongue in sack. For my part, the sea cannot drown me. I swam, ere I could recover the shore, five-and-thirty leagues off and on, by this light. Thou shalt be my lieutenant, 15 monster, or my standard.

Trin. Your lieutenant, if you list; he's no standard.

Ste. We'll not run, Monsieur Monster.

Trin. Nor go neither; but you'll lie like dogs, and yet say nothing neither. 20

Ste. Mooncalf, speak once in thy life, if thou beest a good mooncalf.

Cal. How does thy honor? Let me lick thy shoe. I'll not serve him; he is not valiant.

Trin. Thou liest, most ignorant monster! I am in 25 case to justle a constable. Why, thou deboshed fish thou, was there ever man a coward that hath drunk so much sack as I today? Wilt thou tell a monstrous lie, being but half a fish and half a monster?

Cal. Lo, how he mocks me! Wilt thou let him, my 30
    lord?

Trin. "Lord" quoth he? That a monster should be such a natural!

Cal. Lo, lo, again! Bite him to death I prithee.

Ste. Trinculo, keep a good tongue in your head. 35 If you prove a mutineer—the next tree! The poor monster's my subject, and he shall not suffer indignity.

Cal. I thank my noble lord. Wilt thou be pleased To hearken once again to the suit I made to thee? 40

Ste. Marry, will I. Kneel and repeat it; I will stand, and so shall Trinculo.

60. **compassed:** achieved.

65. **pied ninny:** parti-colored fool. The traditional jester's dress was multicolored; **patch:** another name for fool.

69. **quick freshes:** active springs of fresh water.

Enter Ariel, invisible.

Cal. As I told thee before, I am subject to a tyrant,
A sorcerer, that by his cunning hath
Cheated me of the island.　　　　　　　　　　　　　　45

Ariel. Thou liest.

Cal.　　　　　Thou liest, thou jesting monkey thou!
I would my valiant master would destroy thee.
I do not lie.

Ste. Trinculo, if you trouble him any more in's　　50
tale, by this hand, I will supplant some of your teeth.

Trin. Why, I said nothing.

Ste. Mum then, and no more.—Proceed.

Cal. I say by sorcery he got this isle;
From me he got it. If thy greatness will　　　　　55
Revenge it on him—for I know thou darest,
But this thing dare not—

Ste. That's most certain.

Cal. Thou shalt be lord of it, and I'll serve thee.

Ste. How now shall this be compassed?　　　　60
Canst thou bring me to the party?

Cal. Yea, yea, my lord! I'll yield him thee asleep,
Where thou mayst knock a nail into his head.

Ariel. Thou liest; thou canst not.

Cal. What a pied ninny's this! Thou scurvy patch!　65
I do beseech thy greatness give him blows
And take his bottle from him. When that's gone,
He shall drink naught but brine, for I'll not show him
Where the quick freshes are.

72. **stockfish:** dried and salted fish that had to be beaten to soften it before it was cooked. In other words, Stephano threatens to beat Trinculo as though he were a **stockfish.**

82. **murrain:** plague; literally, a cattle disease.

93. **paunch:** stab, or disembowel.

94. **weasand:** windpipe.

96. **sot:** blockhead.

98. **rootedly:** firmly.

99. **brave utensils:** splendid household furnishings.

Ste. Trinculo, run into no further danger. Interrupt 70
the monster one word further and, by this hand, I'll
turn my mercy out o' doors and make a stockfish of
thee.

Trin. Why, what did I? I did nothing. I'll go farther off. 75

Ste. Didst thou not say he lied?

Ariel. Thou liest.

Ste. Do I so? Take thou that! [*Strikes Trinculo.*]
As you like this, give me the lie another time.

Trin. I did not give thee the lie. Out o' your wits, 80
and hearing too? A pox o' your bottle! This can sack
and drinking do. A murrain on your monster, and the
Devil take your fingers!

Cal. Ha, ha, ha!

Ste. Now forward with your tale.—Prithee stand 85
further off.

Cal. Beat him enough. After a little time
I'll beat him too.

Ste.   Stand farther.—Come, proceed.

Cal. Why, as I told thee, 'tis a custom with him 90
I' the afternoon to sleep. There thou mayst brain him,
Having first seized his books, or with a log
Batter his skull, or paunch him with a stake,
Or cut his weasand with thy knife. Remember
First to possess his books; for without them 95
He's but a sot, as I am, nor hath not
One spirit to command. They all do hate him
As rootedly as I. Burn but his books.
He has brave utensils (for so he calls them)

122. **troll the catch:** sing the round.
123. **whilere:** a while ago.
124. **reason:** anything reasonable.
126. **Flout:** mock; **scout:** deride.
128. **Thought is free:** a proverbial expression.

Which, when he has a house, he'll deck withal.   100
And that most deeply to consider is
The beauty of his daughter. He himself
Calls her a nonpareil. I never saw a woman
But only Sycorax my dam and she;
But she as far surpasseth Sycorax   105
As great'st does least.

　　Ste.　　　　　　Is it so brave a lass?

　　Cal. Ay, lord. She will become thy bed, I warrant,
And bring thee forth brave brood.

　　Ste. Monster, I will kill this man. His daughter and 110
I will be king and queen, save our Graces! and Trinculo and thyself shall be viceroys. Dost thou like the
plot, Trinculo?

　　Trin. Excellent.

　　Ste. Give me thy hand. I am sorry I beat thee; but 115
while thou livest, keep a good tongue in thy head.

　　Cal. Within this half hour will he be asleep.
Wilt thou destroy him then?

　　Ste.　　　　　　Ay, on mine honor.

　　Ariel. This will I tell my master.   120

　　Cal. Thou makest me merry; I am full of pleasure.
Let us be jocund. Will you troll the catch
You taught me but whilere?

　　Ste. At thy request, monster, I will do reason, any
reason. Come on, Trinculo, let us sing.   *Sings.* 125

　　　　　　　Flout 'em and scout 'em
　　　　　　　And scout 'em and flout 'em!
　　　　　　　Thought is free.

S.D. after l. 129. **tabor and pipe:** small drum and fife.

131-32. **the picture of Nobody:** the old play *Nobody and Somebody* (1606) bore a picture on the title page of a man whose body consisted of head and limbs.

The picture of Nobody.
From *Nobody and Somebody* (1606?).

Cal. That's not the tune.

         Ariel plays the tune on a tabor and pipe.

Ste. What is this same?   130

Trin. This is the tune of our catch, played by the picture of Nobody.

Ste. If thou beest a man, show thyself in thy likeness. If thou beest a devil, take 't as thou list.

Trin. O, forgive me my sins!   135

Ste. He that dies pays all debts. I defy thee. Mercy upon us!

Cal. Art thou afeard?

Ste. No, monster, not I.

Cal. Be not afeard. The isle is full of noises,   140
Sounds, and sweet airs that give delight and hurt not.
Sometimes a thousand twangling instruments
Will hum about mine ears; and sometime voices
That, if I then had waked after long sleep,
Will make me sleep again; and then, in dreaming,   145
The clouds methought would open and show riches
Ready to drop upon me, that, when I waked,
I cried to dream again.

Ste. This will prove a brave kingdom to me, where
I shall have my music for nothing.   150

Cal. When Prospero is destroyed.

Ste. That shall be by-and-by. I remember the story.

Trin. The sound is going away. Let's follow it, and after do our work.

Ste. Lead, monster; we'll follow. I would I could 155
see this taborer! He lays it on.

Trin. Wilt come? I'll follow Stephano.

                  Exeunt.

III. iii. Elsewhere on the island Alonso and his party are shown a series of illusory spectacles performed by spirits. Then Ariel lectures them on their sins and counsels repentance and a changed life if they are to escape the wrath of the heavens. Alonso, deeply affected, resolves to find his son even if he has to seek him in the ocean's depths. The good Gonzalo follows his King, intent on preserving him from the possible effects of his desperation.

⁓⁓⁓⁓⁓⁓⁓⁓⁓⁓⁓⁓⁓⁓⁓

1. **By'r Lakin:** by our little lady (the Virgin Mary).

2. **maze:** shrubbery planted in intricate, interweaving patterns; also, a winding dance step. Gonzalo means that he feels they have been going round and round through this unknown territory.

3. **forthrights:** straight lines; **meanders:** winding patterns; **By your patience:** if you will bear with me.

6. **attached:** seized.

7. **To the dulling of my spirits:** with consequent ebbing of my vitality (vital spirits).

11. **frustrate:** frustrated.

17. **throughly:** thoroughly.

19. **oppressed:** overpowered; i.e., worn out.

S.D. after l. 22. **on the top:** probably on the upper stage.

Scene III. [Another part of the island.]

Enter Alonso, Sebastian, Antonio, Gonzalo,
Adrian, Francisco, etc.

Gon. By'r Lakin, I can go no further, sir!
My old bones ache. Here's a maze trod indeed
Through forthrights and meanders. By your patience,
I needs must rest me.
    Alon.   Old lord, I cannot blame thee,   5
Who am myself attached with weariness
To the dulling of my spirits. Sit down and rest.
Even here I will put off my hope, and keep it
No longer for my flatterer. He is drowned
Whom thus we stray to find; and the sea mocks   10
Our frustrate search on land. Well, let him go.
    Ant. [*Aside to Sebastian*] I am right glad that he's
      so out of hope.
Do not for one repulse forego the purpose
That you resolved t' effect.   15
    Seb. [*Aside to Antonio*] The next advantage
Will we take throughly.
    Ant. [*Aside to Sebastian*] Let it be tonight;
For, now they are oppressed with travel, they
Will not nor cannot use such vigilance   20
As when they are fresh.
    Seb. [*Aside to Antonio*] I say tonight. No more.

Solemn and strange music; and Prospero on the
top (invisible).

26. **Give us kind keepers, heavens:** i.e., heaven protect us.

28. **drollery:** puppet show.

29-30. **in Arabia/There is one tree, the phoenix' throne:** the legendary phoenix was said to inhabit Arabia and to be only one in number. When the bird felt death near, it consumed itself on a funeral pyre and was resurrected from its own ashes.

33. **what does else:** whatever else; **want credit:** lack belief.

39. **certes:** certainly.

47. **muse:** wonder at.

The phoenix.
From Claude Paradin, *Devises heroiques* (1557).

Alon. What harmony is this? My good friends,
　hark!

Gon. Marvelous sweet music! 　　　　　　　25

*Enter several strange Shapes, bringing in a banquet;
and dance about it with gentle actions of salutations;
and, inviting the King, etc., to eat, they depart.*

Alon. Give us kind keepers, heavens! What were
　these?

Seb. A living drollery. Now I will believe
That there are unicorns; that in Arabia
There is one tree, the phoenix' throne, one phoenix 　30
At this hour reigning there.

Ant. 　　　　　　　　I'll believe both;
And what does else want credit, come to me,
And I'll be sworn 'tis true. Travelers ne'er did lie,
Though fools at home condemn 'em. 　　　　　35

Gon. 　　　　　　　　If in Naples
I should report this now, would they believe me?
If I should say, I saw such islanders
(For certes these are people of the island),
Who, though they are of monstrous shape, yet, note, 　40
Their manners are more gentle, kind, than of
Our human generation you shall find
Many—nay, almost any.

Pros. [*Aside*] 　　　　Honest lord,
Thou hast said well; for some of you there present 　45
Are worse than devils.

Alon. 　　　　　I cannot too much muse

48. **gesture:** deportment.

51. **Praise in departing:** the proverb "Praise at parting." In other words, "The end crowns all"; it is unwise to judge a matter until it is concluded.

60-1. **mountaineers/Dewlapped like bulls:** possibly a reference to residents of mountain regions of Switzerland where goiter is a common affliction. There were other travelers' tales, however, of monkey-men with folds of flesh at the throat in which they kept their food.

63-4. **men/Whose heads stood in their breasts:** another monstrosity beloved of travel writers. See also *Othello*, I. iii. 160-61.

66. **putter-out of five for one:** investor in voyages at an anticipated return of five for one.

68. **stand to:** i.e., apply myself with a will.

S.D. after l. 71. **like a harpy:** a fabulous monster with a woman's head and face and a bird's wings and claws; in classical mythology, sometimes the agent of divine vengeance; **quaint:** ingenious; clever; see I. ii. 388.

73. **hath to instrument:** manipulates.

"Men whose heads stood in their breasts."
From John Mandeville, *Voyages and Travels* (1583?).

Such shapes, such gesture, and such sound, expressing
(Although they want the use of tongue) a kind
Of excellent dumb discourse.   50
  Pros. [*Aside*]   Praise in departing.
  Fran. They vanished strangely.
  Seb.   No matter, since
They have left their viands behind; for we have
    stomachs.   55
Will't please you taste of what is here?
  Alon.   Not I.
  Gon. Faith, sir, you need not fear. When we were
    boys,
Who would believe that there were mountaineers   60
Dewlapped like bulls, whose throats had hanging at
    'em
Wallets of flesh? or that there were such men
Whose heads stood in their breasts? which now we
    find   65
Each putter-out of five for one will bring us
Good warrant of.
  Alon.   I will stand to, and feed;
Although my last, no matter, since I feel
The best is past. Brother, my lord the Duke,   70
Stand to, and do as we.

*Thunder and lightning. Enter Ariel, like a harpy;
claps his wings upon the table; and with a quaint
          device the banquet vanishes.*

  Ariel. You are three men of sin, whom destiny—
That hath to instrument this lower world

74. **never-surfeited sea:** i.e., the insatiable sea was forced by destiny to disgorge the three men; otherwise they would have been lost.

79. **proper:** emphatic: own.

83. **bemocked-at stabs:** i.e., ineffectual wounds.

84. **still-closing:** ever-closing; i.e., closing as soon as stabbed.

85. **dowle:** small, soft feather.

87. **massy:** heavy.

91. **requit it:** requited your deed (by its treatment of you).

97. **perdition:** destruction.

99. **whose wraths:** i.e., the wraths of the powers of heaven.

102. **clear:** blameless.

And what is in't—the never-surfeited sea
Hath caused to belch up you, and on this island,   75
Where man doth not inhabit—you 'mongst men
Being most unfit to live. I have made you mad;
And even with suchlike valor men hang and drown
Their proper selves.
          [*Alonso, Sebastian, etc., draw their swords.*]
                    You fools! I and my fellows   80
Are ministers of Fate. The elements,
Of whom your swords are tempered, may as well
Wound the loud winds, or with bemocked-at stabs
Kill the still-closing waters, as diminish
One dowle that's in my plume. My fellow ministers   85
Are like invulnerable. If you could hurt,
Your swords are now too massy for your strengths
And will not be uplifted. But remember
(For that's my business to you) that you three
From Milan did supplant good Prospero;   90
Exposed unto the sea, which hath requit it,
Him and his innocent child; for which foul deed
The powers, delaying (not forgetting), have
Incensed the seas and shores, yea, all the creatures,
Against your peace. Thee of thy son, Alonso,   95
They have bereft; and do pronounce by me
Ling'ring perdition (worse than any death
Can be at once) shall step by step attend
You and your ways; whose wraths to guard you from,
Which here, in this most desolate isle, else falls   100
Upon your heads, is nothing but heart's sorrow
And a clear life ensuing.

103. **Bravely:** excellently; see III. ii. 107 and 149 and other similar uses.

105. **a grace it had, devouring:** i.e., the harpy, as portrayed by Ariel, had a certain grace in disposing of the banquet.

106. **bated:** abated; omitted; see II. i. 103.

107. **good life:** lifelike realism.

108. **observation strange:** extraordinary care. In the context this may refer to the way in which the spirits pantomimed their roles as servants, or to the care with which they followed his instructions; **meaner ministers:** spirits of a lower order than Ariel.

109. **Their several kinds:** i.e., the functions appropriate to each.

110. **knit up:** tangled up.

118. **monstrous:** outrageously abnormal or unnatural.

122. **bass my trespass:** intone my sin in a bass voice.

127. **their legions o'er:** legions of devils to the last one. See Mark 5:9.

He vanishes in thunder; then, to soft music, enter the Shapes again, and dance, with mocks and mows, and carrying out the table.

  Pros. [*Aside*] Bravely the figure of this harpy hast
    thou
Performed, my Ariel; a grace it had, devouring.   105
Of my instruction hast thou nothing bated
In what thou hadst to say. So, with good life
And observation strange, my meaner ministers
Their several kinds have done. My high charms work,
And these, mine enemies, are all knit up   110
In their distractions. They now are in my pow'r;
And in these fits I leave them, while I visit
Young Ferdinand, whom they suppose is drowned,
And his and mine loved darling.   [*Exit above.*]
  Gon. I' the name of something holy, sir, why stand 115
    you
In this strange stare?
  Alon.   O, it is monstrous, monstrous!
Methought the billows spoke and told me of it;
The winds did sing it to me; and the thunder,   120
That deep and dreadful organ pipe, pronounced
The name of Prosper. It did bass my trespass.
Therefore my son i' the ooze is bedded; and
I'll seek him deeper than e'er plummet sounded
And with him there lie mudded.   *Exit.* 125
  Seb.   But one fiend at a time,
I'll fight their legions o'er!

132. **bite the spirits:** assault their vital spirits; see l. 7.

134. **ecstasy:** madness.

Iris.

From Vincenzo Cartari, *Imagini de gli dei delli antichi* (1615).
(See IV. i. 68)

Ant.   I'll be thy second.

        Exeunt [Sebastian and Antonio].

  Gon. All three of them are desperate. Their great guilt,   130

Like poison given to work a great time after,

Now 'gins to bite the spirits. I do beseech you,

That are of suppler joints, follow them swiftly

And hinder them from what this ecstasy

May now provoke them to.   135

  Adr.   Follow, I pray you.

        Exeunt omnes.

THE TEMPEST

ACT IV

IV. i. Prospero, satisfied with Ferdinand, promises Miranda to him. He orders Ariel to arrange a spectacle for the two lovers. Spirits in the forms of Iris, Ceres, and Juno promise them the blessings of a happy marriage. The spell is broken, however, when Prospero remembers Caliban's conspiracy. Ariel reports that he left the three plotters vainly dancing in a stinking pond, and Prospero orders him to place some garments on a tree outside his cell. Stephano and Trinculo cannot resist the cheap finery, though Caliban tries to persuade them to leave it alone and get on with the murder of Prospero. Prospero and Ariel then set spirits in the shape of hounds to hunt them, while goblins torment them.

||||||||||||||||||||||||||||||||

3. **a third of mine own life:** that is, his daughter Miranda.

7. **strangely:** to an exceptional degree; see **strange,** III. iii. 108.

9. **boast her off:** present her boastfully.

13. **Against an oracle:** even if the voice of superhuman wisdom should deny my belief.

15. **purchased:** acquired.

17. **sanctimonious:** sanctified; holy.

ACT IV

Scene I. [Before Prospero's cell.]

Enter Prospero, Ferdinand, and Miranda.

Pros. If I have too austerely punished you,
Your compensation makes amends; for I
Have given you here a third of mine own life,
Or that for which I live; who once again
I tender to thy hand. All thy vexations   5
Were but my trials of thy love, and thou
Hast strangely stood the test. Here, afore heaven,
I ratify this my rich gift. O Ferdinand,
Do not smile at me that I boast her off,
For thou shalt find she will outstrip all praise   10
And make it halt behind her.

Fer.   I do believe it
Against an oracle.

Pros. Then, as my gift, and thine own acquisition
Worthily purchased, take my daughter. But   15
If thou dost break her virgin-knot before
All sanctimonious ceremonies may

19. **aspersion:** besprinkling as a benediction.

20. **contract grow:** betrothal grow into marriage.

24. **As Hymen's lamp shall light you:** as you hope that Hymen, god of marriage, will illuminate your wedding festivities vividly with his torch, omen of a happy married life.

28. **suggestion:** evil temptation, as at II. i. 328.

29. **Our worser genius can:** that our worser nature can offer.

32. **or:** either; **Phoebus' steeds:** the horses pulling the chariot of the sun god; **foundered:** lamed.

Hymen.
From Vincenzo Cartari, *Imagini de gli dei delli antichi* (1615).

With full and holy rite be minist'red,
No sweet aspersion shall the heavens let fall
To make this contract grow; but barren hate,   20
Sour-eyed disdain, and discord shall bestrew
The union of your bed with weeds so loathly
That you shall hate it both. Therefore take heed,
As Hymen's lamp shall light you!
   Fer.   As I hope   25
For quiet days, fair issue, and long life,
With such love as 'tis now, the murkiest den,
The most opportune place, the strong'st suggestion
Our worser genius can, shall never melt
Mine honor into lust, to take away   30
The edge of that day's celebration
When I shall think or Phoebus' steeds are foundered
Or Night kept chained below.
   Pros.   Fairly spoke.
Sit then and talk with her; she is thine own.   35
What, Ariel! my industrious servant, Ariel!

Enter Ariel.

   Ariel. What would my potent master? Here I am.
   Pros. Thou and thy meaner fellows your last
    service
Did worthily perform; and I must use you   40
In such another trick. Go bring the rabble,
O'er whom I give thee pow'r, here to this place.
Incite them to quick motion; for I must
Bestow upon the eyes of this young couple

45. **Some vanity of mine art:** a trivial demonstration of my magic art.

47. **Presently:** at once.

48. **with a twink:** in a twinkling.

52. **mop and mow:** grimaces; see **mow** in S.D. at III. iii. 102.

56. **conceive:** understand.

57. **true:** faithful to his promise.

63. **liver:** the organ responsible for passion.

65. **corollary:** surplus; i.e., more spirits than needed.

66. **want a spirit:** have one less spirit than needed; **pertly:** briskly; quickly.

S.D. after l. 67. **Iris:** i.e., a spirit representing Iris, personification of the rainbow and messenger of the gods according to some classical authorities.

68. **Ceres:** goddess of plenty; **leas:** meadows.

69. **fetches:** vetches; a hay plant.

71. **thatched:** covered; **stover:** hay or grass grown to provide winter feed for cattle; **them to keep:** i.e., to feed the sheep.

Some vanity of mine art. It is my promise,   45
And they expect it from me.

   Ariel.   Presently?

   Pros. Ay, with a twink.

   Ariel. Before you can say "Come" and "Go,"

And breathe twice and cry, "So, so,"   50

Each one, tripping on his toe,

Will be here with mop and mow.

Do you love me master? No?

   Pros. Dearly, my delicate Ariel. Do not approach

Till thou dost hear me call.   55

   Ariel.   Well! I conceive.   *Exit.*

   Pros. Look thou be true. Do not give dalliance

Too much the rein. The strongest oaths are straw

To the fire i' the blood. Be more abstemious,

Or else good night your vow!   60

   Fer.   I warrant you, sir.

The white cold virgin snow upon my heart

Abates the ardor of my liver.

   Pros.   Well.

Now come, my Ariel! Bring a corollary   65

Rather than want a spirit. Appear, and pertly!

No tongue! All eyes! Be silent.   *Soft music.*

Enter Iris.

   Iris. Ceres, most bounteous lady, thy rich leas

Of wheat, rye, barley, fetches, oats, and pease;

Thy turfy mountains, where live nibbling sheep,   70

And flat meads thatched with stover, them to keep;

72. **pioned and twilled:** perhaps, trenched and ridged. The passage is obscure and scholars have debated the meaning of the words. **Pioned** may come from the same stem as the word "pioneer" (digger or miner).

73. **betrims:** i.e., with flowers.

76. **dismissed bachelor:** rejected lover.

77. **lasslorn:** bereaved of his sweetheart; **pole-clipt vineyard:** vineyard, the vines of which twine on poles. **Clipt** equals "embraced."

78. **sea-marge:** seashore.

79. **air:** air yourself; take an airing; **queen o' the sky:** Juno.

80. **wat'ry arch:** rainbow; see S.D. after l. 67.

S.D. after l. 81. **Juno descends:** This stage direction in the Folio has puzzled editors, who feel that it is too early for Juno to appear. It was customary for Elizabethan directors to have the gods come down from a trap door in the "heavens" in a machine, and Juno may have been let down in such a device.

83. **peacocks:** fowl sacred to Juno; **amain:** apace; at a fast pace.

84. **entertain:** welcome.

90. **bosky:** woody; wooded; **down:** open expanse of upland.

94. **estate:** bestow.

Thy banks with pioned and twilled brims,
Which spongy April at thy hest betrims
To make cold nymphs chaste crowns; and thy broom
    groves,   75
Whose shadow the dismissed bachelor loves,
Being lasslorn; thy pole-clipt vineyard;
And thy sea-marge, sterile and rocky-hard,
Where thou thyself dost air—the queen o' the sky,
Whose wat'ry arch and messenger am I,   80
Bids thee leave these, and with her sovereign Grace,
                      Juno descends.
Here on this grass-plot, in this very place,
To come and sport. Her peacocks fly amain;
Approach, rich Ceres, her to entertain.

              Enter Ceres.

  Ceres. Hail, many-colored messenger, that ne'er   85
Dost disobey the wife of Jupiter,
Who, with thy saffron wings, upon my flow'rs
Diffusest honey drops, refreshing show'rs,
And with each end of thy blue bow dost crown
My bosky acres and my unshrubbed down,   90
Rich scarf to my proud earth—why hath thy queen
Summoned me hither to this short-grassed green?
  Iris. A contract of true love to celebrate
And some donation freely to estate
On the blest lovers.   95
  Ceres.   Tell me, heavenly bow,
If Venus or her son, as thou dost know,
Do now attend the queen. Since they did plot

99. **dusky Dis my daughter got:** i.e., Pluto, king of the underworld kidnaped Ceres' daughter Proserpina. See Ovid, *Metamorphoses*, Book V.

100. **her blind boy:** i.e., Venus' son Cupid; **scandaled:** scandalous.

103. **Deity:** Divine Majesty.

104. **Paphos:** a town in Cyprus where Venus is fabled to have landed, thereafter a center of her worship.

105. **Dove-drawn:** the chariot of Venus was said to be drawn by doves.

110. **Mars's hot minion:** i.e., Venus, who once had an amour with the god Mars. **Minion** means "mistress" or "darling."

111. **waspish-headed:** ill-tempered.

113. **right out:** completely; that is, he will settle down to be a mere boy instead of a god.

121. **still:** ever.

The abduction of Proserpina.
From Claude Menestrier, *L'art des emblemes* (1684).

The means that dusky Dis my daughter got,
Her and her blind boy's scandaled company 100
I have forsworn.
  Iris.   Of her society
Be not afraid. I met her Deity
Cutting the clouds towards Paphos, and her son
Dove-drawn with her. Here thought they to have 105
    done
Some wanton charm upon this man and maid,
Whose vows are, that no bed-right shall be paid
Till Hymen's torch be lighted; but in vain.
Mars's hot minion is returned again; 110
Her waspish-headed son has broke his arrows,
Swears he will shoot no more, but play with sparrows
And be a boy right out.

[Enter Juno.]

  Ceres.   Highest queen of state,
Great Juno, comes; I know her by her gait. 115
  Juno. How does my bounteous sister? Go with me
To bless this twain, that they may prosperous be
And honored in their issue.

They sing.

  Juno.   Honor, riches, marriage blessing,
        Long continuance, and increasing, 120
        Hourly joys be still upon you!
        Juno sings her blessings on you.

123. **foison:** abundance (of crops); see II. i. 177.

127-28. **Spring come to you at the farthest/In the very end of harvest:** i.e., may spring follow autumn immediately, no winter intervening.

138. **So rare a wond'red father and a wise:** i.e., a father so wise and rarely wonderful.

144. **wind'ring:** probably, winding.

146. **sedged crowns:** heads crowned with sedge, a plant growing in marshy soil.

147. **crisp:** curly; i.e., rippling.

Ceres.
From Vincenzo Cartari, *Imagini de gli dei delli antichi* (1615).

Ceres. Earth's increase, foison plenty,
          Barns and garners never empty,
          Vines with clust'ring bunches growing,   125
          Plants with goodly burden bowing;
          Spring come to you at the farthest
          In the very end of harvest!
          Scarcity and want shall shun you,
          Ceres' blessing so is on you.   130

Fer. This is a most majestic vision, and
Harmonious charmingly. May I be bold
To think these spirits?
Pros.   Spirits, which by mine art
I have from their confines called to enact   135
My present fancies.
Fer.   Let me live here ever!
So rare a wond'red father and a wise
Makes this place Paradise.

          *Juno and Ceres whisper, and send Iris
                              on employment.*

Pros.   Sweet now, silence!   140
Juno and Ceres whisper seriously.
There's something else to do. Hush and be mute,
Or else our spell is marred.
Iris. You nymphs, called Naiads, of the wind'ring
          brooks,   145
With your sedged crowns and ever-harmless looks,
Leave your crisp channels, and on this green land
Answer your summons. Juno does command.
Come, temperate nymphs, and help to celebrate
A contract of true love. Be not too late.   150

S.D. after l. 155. **heavily:** slowly and dispiritedly.

159. **Avoid:** avaunt; be off.

161. **passion:** storm of emotion. The word was used for any strong feeling; see I. ii. 478.

164. **anger so distempered:** such violent anger.

165. **in a moved sort:** i.e., distressed.

170. **baseless:** i.e., lacking real foundation; insubstantial.

Juno.

From Vincenzo Cartari, *Imagini de gli dei delli antichi* (1615).

Enter certain Nymphs.

You sunburned sicklemen, of August weary,
Come hither from the furrow and be merry.
Make holiday. Your rye-straw hats put on,
And these fresh nymphs encounter every one
In country footing.   155

*Enter certain Reapers, properly habited. They join
with the Nymphs in a graceful dance; towards the
end whereof Prospero starts suddenly and speaks;
after which, to a strange, hollow, and confused noise,
they heavily vanish.*

    Pros. [*Aside*] I had forgot that foul conspiracy
Of the beast Caliban and his confederates
Against my life. The minute of their plot
Is almost come.—[*To the Spirits*] Well done! Avoid!
    No more!   160
    Fer. This is strange. Your father's in some passion
That works him strongly.
    Mir.   Never till this day
Saw I him touched with anger so distempered.
    Pros. You do look, my son, in a moved sort,   165
As if you were dismayed. Be cheerful, sir.
Our revels now are ended. These our actors,
As I foretold you, were all spirits and
Are melted into air, into thin air;
And, like the baseless fabric of this vision,   170
The cloud-capped towers, the gorgeous palaces,

173. **all which it inherit:** all earthly creatures. Prospero is saying that life itself is as illusory as the magic show he has just evoked.

174. **pageant:** spectacle.

175. **rack:** wisp of cloud.

176. **on:** of.

180. **If you be pleased:** if it please you to do so.

184. **Come with a thought:** that is, he has come at the instant of my thought.

186. **Thy thoughts I cleave to:** that is, I am firmly attached to your thoughts, so that when you think of me I am instantly by your side.

193. **varlets:** rogues.

198. **bending:** aiming themselves.

The solemn temples, the great globe itself,
Yea, all which it inherit, shall dissolve,
And, like this insubstantial pageant faded,
Leave not a rack behind. We are such stuff   175
As dreams are made on, and our little life
Is rounded with a sleep. Sir, I am vexed.
Bear with my weakness. My old brain is troubled.
Be not disturbed with my infirmity.
If you be pleased, retire into my cell   180
And there repose. A turn or two I'll walk
To still my beating mind.

    Fer. } We wish your peace.   *Exeunt.*
    Mir.

Enter Ariel.

  Pros. Come with a thought! I thank thee, Ariel.
    Come.   185
  Ariel. Thy thoughts I cleave to. What's thy pleasure?
  Pros. Spirit, we must prepare to meet with Caliban.
  Ariel. Ay, my commander. When I presented
    Ceres,
I thought to have told thee of it, but I feared   190
Lest I might anger thee.
  Pros. Say again, where didst thou leave these
    varlets?
  Ariel. I told you, sir, they were redhot with drink-
    ing;   195
So full of valor that they smote the air
For breathing in their faces, beat the ground
For kissing of their feet; yet always bending

201. **Advanced:** raised.

204. **goss:** gorse, another name for **furze,** which is a spiny plant.

207. **mantled:** covered with scum.

212. **trumpery:** trifles.

213. **stale:** bait.

216. **Nurture:** moral training or discipline.

219. **cankers:** festers with malice.

221. **line:** lime or linden tree.

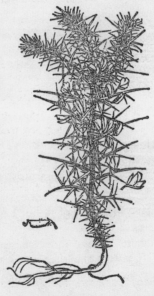

Furze.
From Rembert Dodoens, A *New Herbal* (1578).

Towards their project. Then I beat my tabor;
At which like unbacked colts they pricked their ears, 200
Advanced their eyelids, lifted up their noses
As they smelt music. So I charmed their ears
That calf-like they my lowing followed through
Toothed briers, sharp furzes, pricking goss, and
    thorns,   205
Which ent'red their frail shins. At last I left them
I' the filthy mantled pool beyond your cell,
There dancing up to the chins, that the foul lake
O'erstunk their feet.

Pros.   This was well done, my bird. 210
Thy shape invisible retain thou still.
The trumpery in my house, go bring it hither
For stale to catch these thieves.

Ariel.   I go, I go.   *Exit.*

Pros. A devil, a born devil, on whose nature 215
Nurture can never stick! on whom my pains,
Humanely taken, all, all lost, quite lost!
And as with age his body uglier grows,
So his mind cankers. I will plague them all,
Even to roaring.   220

   Enter Ariel, loaden with glistening apparel, etc.

       Come, hang them on this line.
      [*Prospero and Ariel remain, invisible.*]

   Enter Caliban, Stephano, and Trinculo, all wet.

   Cal. Pray you tread softly, that the blind mole may
    not
Hear a foot fall. We now are near his cell.

226. **Jack:** knave.

232. **wert:** would be.

235. **hoodwink:** cover from sight; blot out.

243. **fetch off:** rescue.

247. **good mischief:** evil deed which will result in your good fortune.

252-53. **King Stephano . . . peer . . . worthy Stephano:** Trinculo is thinking of a ballad, beginning "King Stephen was and a worthy peer," and ending, "Then take thy old cloak about thee," also quoted in *Othello*, II. iii. 84-91.

Ste. Monster, your fairy, which you say is a harm- 225
less fairy, has done little better than played the Jack
with us.

Trin. Monster, I do smell all horse-piss, at which
my nose is in great indignation.

Ste. So is mine. Do you hear, monster? If I should 230
take a displeasure against you, look you—

Trin. Thou wert but a lost monster.

Cal. Good my lord, give me thy favor still.
Be patient, for the prize I'll bring thee to
Shall hoodwink this mischance. Therefore speak 235
    softly.
All's hushed as midnight yet.

Trin. Ay, but to lose our bottles in the pool—

Ste. There is not only disgrace and dishonor in
that, monster, but an infinite loss.   240

Trin. That's more to me than my wetting. Yet this
is your harmless fairy, monster.

Ste. I will fetch off my bottle, though I be o'er ears
for my labor.

Cal. Prithee, my king, be quiet. Seest thou here? 245
This is the mouth o' the cell. No noise, and enter.
Do that good mischief which may make this island
Thine own forever, and I, thy Caliban,
For aye thy foot-licker.

Ste. Give me thy hand. I do begin to have bloody 250
    thoughts.

Trin. O King Stephano! O peer! O worthy Stephano, look what a wardrobe here is for thee!

Cal. Let it alone, thou fool! It is but trash.

255-56. **what belongs to a frippery:** what is suitable for an old clothes shop.

262. **luggage:** worthless burden.

267. **jerkin:** jacket.

268. **line:** a term for the Equator. Sailors who made the voyage across the equatorial line frequently suffered from scurvy and there are numerous references to the resultant loss of hair. The jerkin is presumably trimmed with fur.

270. **by line and level:** with methodical accuracy, with a pun.

275. **pass of pate:** thrust of wit; jest. A **pass** is literally a fencing thrust.

276. **lime:** birdlime, a gluey substance used to snare birds.

277. **away with the rest:** i.e., hold fast to the rest of the clothing.

278. **on't:** of it; **time:** opportunity.

279. **barnacles:** barnacle geese, which were popularly believed to grow from the shellfish; i.e., monstrosities.

280. **villainous:** wretchedly.

283. **Go to:** come on, get on with it.

Trin. O ho, monster! we know what belongs to a   255
frippery. O King Stephano!

Ste. Put off that gown, Trinculo. By this hand, I'll
have that gown!

Trin. Thy Grace shall have it.

Cal. The dropsy drown this fool! What do you   260
    mean
To dote thus on such luggage? Let't alone,
And do the murder first. If he awake,
From toe to crown he'll fill our skins with pinches,
Make us strange stuff.   265

Ste. Be you quiet, monster. Mistress line, is not
this my jerkin? [*Takes it down.*] Now is the jerkin
under the line. Now, jerkin, you are like to lose your
hair and prove a bald jerkin.

Trin. Do, do! We steal by line and level, an't like   270
your Grace.

Ste. I thank thee for that jest. Here's a garment
for't. Wit shall not go unrewarded while I am king
of this country. "Steal by line and level" is an excellent pass of pate. There's another garment for't.   275

Trin. Monster, come put some lime upon your fingers, and away with the rest!

Cal. I will have none on't. We shall lose our time
And all be turned to barnacles, or to apes
With foreheads villainous low.   280

Ste. Monster, lay-to your fingers. Help to bear this
away where my hogshead of wine is, or I'll turn you
out of my kingdom. Go to, carry this.

Trin. And this.

Ste. Ay, and this.   285

291. **aged cramps:** the cramps of old age.

293. **pard:** leopard; **cat o' mountain:** catamount; panther.

A noise of hunters heard. Enter divers Spirits in shape of dogs and hounds, hunting them about, Prospero and Ariel setting them on.

Pros. Hey, Mountain, hey!

Ariel. Silver! there it goes, Silver!

Pros. Fury, Fury! There, Tyrant, there! Hark, hark!
    [*Caliban, Stephano, and Trinculo are driven out.*]
Go, charge my goblins that they grind their joints
With dry convulsions, shorten up their sinews   290
With aged cramps, and more pinch-spotted make
    them
Than pard or cat o' mountain.

Ariel.   Hark, they roar.

Pros. Let them be hunted soundly. At this hour   295
Lie at my mercy all mine enemies.
Shortly shall all my labors end, and thou
Shalt have the air at freedom. For a little
Follow, and do me service.

                              Exeunt.

THE TEMPEST

ACT V

V. i. Ariel reports to Prospero on his enemies, whose plight is affecting even to a spirit with no human feelings. Prospero is contented with the penitence of his victims and, renouncing his magic, explains all to Alonso and the others. The missing Ferdinand is restored to his father, who also meets Miranda, his future daughter-in-law. The spellbound sailors are released. Prospero sends all aboard the vessel and promises a calm voyage back to Naples. Ariel is at last free to do as he will.

2-3. **crack not:** work perfectly; **Time/Goes upright with his carriage:** Time does not bend in carrying his burden; that is, Prospero's plans are going according to schedule.

12. **line:** linden, as at IV. i. 221; **weather-fends:** shields from the weather.

14. **abide:** remain.

19. **reeds:** thatch.

ACT V

Scene I. [Before the cell of Prospero.]

Enter Prospero in his magic robes, and Ariel.

Pros. Now does my project gather to a head.
My charms crack not, my spirits obey, and Time
Goes upright with his carriage. How's the day?
  Ariel. On the sixth hour, at which time, my lord,
You said our work should cease.   5
  Pros.   I did say so
When first I raised the tempest. Say, my spirit,
How fares the King and 's followers?
  Ariel.   Confined together
In the same fashion as you gave in charge,   10
Just as you left them—all prisoners, sir,
In the line grove which weather-fends your cell.
They cannot budge till your release. The King,
His brother, and yours abide all three distracted,
And the remainder mourning over them,   15
Brimful of sorrow and dismay; but chiefly
Him that you termed, sir, the good old Lord Gonzalo.
His tears run down his beard like winter's drops
From eaves of reeds. Your charm so strongly works 'em,

20. **affections:** feelings.

27-8. **relish all as sharply/Passion:** am as sensitive to strong emotion as.

32-3. **The rarer action is/In virtue than in vengeance:** i.e., it is finer to behave in accordance with noble impulse than with the dictates of vengeance.

40. **standing:** still; having no tide.

43. **demipuppets:** fairies; "little people."

44. **ringlets:** fairy rings.

46. **mushrumps:** mushrooms.

47. **solemn curfew:** the customary nine o'clock curfew bell, supposedly a signal to spirits of all kinds to walk abroad.

That if you now beheld them, your affections   20
Would become tender.

   Pros.   Dost thou think so, spirit?

   Ariel. Mine would, sir, were I human.

   Pros.   And mine shall.

Hast thou, which art but air, a touch, a feeling   25
Of their afflictions, and shall not myself,
One of their kind, that relish all as sharply
Passion as they, be kindlier moved than thou art?
Though with their high wrongs I am struck to the
     quick,   30
Yet with my nobler reason 'gainst my fury
Do I take part. The rarer action is
In virtue than in vengeance. They being penitent,
The sole drift of my purpose doth extend
Not a frown further. Go, release them, Ariel.   35
My charms I'll break, their senses I'll restore,
And they shall be themselves.

   Ariel.   I'll fetch them, sir.   *Exit.*

   Pros. [*Makes a magic circle with his staff*] Ye elves
     of hills, brooks, standing lakes, and groves,   40
And ye that on the sands with printless foot
Do chase the ebbing Neptune, and do fly him
When he comes back; you demipuppets that
By moonshine do the green sour ringlets make,
Whereof the ewe not bites; and you, whose pastime   45
Is to make midnight mushrumps, that rejoice
To hear the solemn curfew; by whose aid
(Weak masters though ye be) I have bedimmed
The noontide sun, called forth the mutinous winds,
And 'twixt the green sea and the azured vault   50

54. **spurs:** roots.

61. **staff:** magic wand.

64. **book:** book of magic spells.

S.D. after l. 64. **gesture:** manner; air.

65. **air:** piece of music; **and:** i.e., which is.

70. **ev'n sociable:** exactly sympathizing with; i.e., in sympathetic accord with.

71. **Fall fellowly drops:** drop companionable tears; **apace:** speedily.

Set roaring war; to the dread rattling thunder
Have I given fire and rifted Jove's stout oak
With his own bolt; the strong-based promontory
Have I made shake and by the spurs plucked up
The pine and cedar; graves at my command   55
Have waked their sleepers, oped, and let 'em forth
By my so potent art. But this rough magic
I here abjure; and when I have required
Some heavenly music (which even now I do)
To work mine end upon their senses that   60
This airy charm is for, I'll break my staff,
Bury it certain fathoms in the earth,
And deeper than did ever plummet sound
I'll drown my book.   *Solemn music.*

*Here enters Ariel before; then Alonso, with a frantic
gesture, attended by Gonzalo; Sebastian and Antonio
in like manner, attended by Adrian and Francisco.
They all enter the circle which Prospero had made,
and there stand charmed; which Prospero observing,
speaks.*

A solemn air, and the best comforter   65
To an unsettled fancy, cure thy brains,
Now useless, boiled within thy skull! There stand,
For you are spell-stopped.
Holy Gonzalo, honorable man,
Mine eyes, ev'n sociable to the show of thine,   70
Fall fellowly drops. The charm dissolves apace;
And as the morning steals upon the night,
Melting the darkness, so their rising senses

74. **ignorant fumes:** fumes of ignorance (mental confusion); **mantle:** cover.

76. **sir:** gentleman.

77-8. **pay thy graces/Home:** repay your favors to me thoroughly.

87-90. **Their understanding/ . . . muddy:** comprehension is approaching flood tide and will soon reach the height of normal reason, covering the muddy flats of stupidity. **Not one:** i.e., there is not one.

92. **rapier:** sword.

93. **discase me:** remove my magician's gown.

94. **sometime Milan:** the former Duke of Milan; see **Absolute Milan,** I. ii. 130.

Begin to chase the ignorant fumes that mantle
Their clearer reason. O good Gonzalo,   75
My true preserver, and a loyal sir
To him thou followst! I will pay thy graces
Home both in word and deed. Most cruelly
Didst thou, Alonso, use me and my daughter.
Thy brother was a furtherer in the act.   80
Thou art pinched for't now, Sebastian. Flesh and
    blood,
You, brother mine, that entertained ambition,
Expelled remorse and nature; who, with Sebastian
(Whose inward pinches therefore are most strong),   85
Would here have killed your king, I do forgive thee,
Unnatural though thou art. Their understanding
Begins to swell, and the approaching tide
Will shortly fill the reasonable shore,
That now lies foul and muddy. Not one of them   90
That yet looks on me or would know me. Ariel,
Fetch me the hat and rapier in my cell.
I will discase me, and myself present
As I was sometime Milan. Quickly, spirit!
Thou shalt ere long be free.   95

        [*Exit Ariel and returns immediately.*]

        Ariel sings and helps to attire him.

        Where the bee sucks, there suck I;
        In a cowslip's bell I lie;
        There I couch when owls do cry.

109. **presently:** at once.

111. **Or ere:** before.

121. **Whe'r:** whether.

122. **enchanted trifle:** apparition conjured of thin air; **abuse:** deceive.

126. **crave:** require.

127. **An if this be:** if this really is.

On the bat's back I do fly
After summer merrily.   100
    Merrily, merrily shall I live now
Under the blossom that hangs on the bough.

Pros. Why, that's my dainty Ariel! I shall miss thee,
But yet thou shalt have freedom. So, so, so.
To the King's ship, invisible as thou art!   105
There shalt thou find the mariners asleep
Under the hatches. The master and the boatswain
Being awake, enforce them to this place,
And presently, I prithee.
    Ariel. I drink the air before me, and return   110
Or ere your pulse twice beat.   *Exit.*
    Gon. All torment, trouble, wonder, and amazement
Inhabits here. Some heavenly power guide us
Out of this fearful country!
    Pros.   Behold, sir King,   115
The wronged Duke of Milan, Prospero.
For more assurance that a living prince
Does now speak to thee, I embrace thy body,
And to thee and thy company I bid
A hearty welcome.   120
    Alon.   Whe'r thou beest he or no,
Or some enchanted trifle to abuse me,
As late I have been, I not know. Thy pulse
Beats, as of flesh and blood; and, since I saw thee,
The affliction of my mind amends, with which,   125
I fear, a madness held me. This must crave
(An if this be at all) a most strange story.

133. **thine age:** your aged self.
138. **subtleties:** hidden and unusual qualities.
143. **justify:** prove.
150. **perforce:** whether you will or no.

Thy dukedom I resign and do entreat
Thou pardon me my wrongs. But how should
    Prospero   130
Be living and be here?
  Pros.   First, noble friend,
Let me embrace thine age, whose honor cannot
Be measured or confined.
  Gon.   Whether this be   135
Or be not, I'll not swear.
  Pros.   You do yet taste
Some subtleties o' the isle, that will not let you
Believe things certain. Welcome, my friends all.
[*Aside to Sebastian and Antonio*] But you, my brace 140
    of lords, were I so minded,
I here could pluck his Highness' frown upon you,
And justify you traitors. At this time
I will tell no tales.
  Seb. [*Aside*]   The Devil speaks in him.   145
  Pros.   No.
For you, most wicked sir, whom to call brother
Would even infect my mouth, I do forgive
Thy rankest fault—all of them; and require
My dukedom of thee, which perforce I know   150
Thou must restore.
  Alon.   If thou beest Prospero,
Give us particulars of thy preservation;
How thou hast met us here, who three hours since
Were wracked upon this shore; where I have lost   155
(How sharp the point of this remembrance is!)
My dear son Ferdinand.

158. **woe:** woeful; cf., "Woe is me."

164. **rest myself content:** remain happy myself.

166-67. **As great to me as late:** a loss as great just as recently; **supportable/To make the dear loss:** i.e., to make the grievous loss bearable.

177. **admire:** wonder.

178. **devour their reason:** i.e., their reason is overwhelmed by their consternation.

179-80. **do offices of truth:** perform truthfully; **their words/Are natural breath:** their efforts at speech result only in astonished gasps.

Pros.   I am woe for't, sir.

Alon. Irreparable is the loss, and patience

Says it is past her cure.   160

    Pros.   I rather think

You have not sought her help, of whose soft grace

For the like loss I have her sovereign aid

And rest myself content.

    Alon.   You the like loss?   165

    Pros. As great to me as late; and, supportable

To make the dear loss, have I means much weaker

Than you may call to comfort you; for I

Have lost my daughter.

    Alon.   A daughter?   170

O heavens, that they were living both in Naples,

The King and Queen there! That they were, I wish

Myself were mudded in that oozy bed

Where my son lies. When did you lose your daughter?   175

    Pros. In this last tempest. I perceive these lords

At this encounter do so much admire

That they devour their reason, and scarce think

Their eyes do offices of truth, their words

Are natural breath. But, howsoev'r you have   180

Been justled from your senses, know for certain

That I am Prospero, and that very duke

Which was thrust forth of Milan, who most strangely

Upon this shore, where you were wracked, was landed   185

To be the lord on't. No more yet of this;

For 'tis a chronicle of day by day,

194. **content:** please.

S.D. after l. 195. **discovers:** reveals (probably by drawing back a curtain, perhaps on the inner stage).

Not a relation for a breakfast, nor
Befitting this first meeting. Welcome, sir.
This cell's my court. Here have I few attendants, 190
And subjects none abroad. Pray you look in.
My dukedom since you have given me again,
I will requite you with as good a thing,
At least bring forth a wonder to content ye
As much as me my dukedom. 195

Here Prospero discovers Ferdinand and Miranda
playing at chess.

Mir. Sweet lord, you play me false.
Fer. No, my dearest love,
I would not for the world.
Mir. Yes, for a score of kingdoms you should
wrangle, 200
And I would call it fair play.
Alon. If this prove
A vision of the island, one dear son
Shall I twice lose.
Seb. A most high miracle! 205
Fer. Though the seas threaten, they are merciful.
I have cursed them without cause. [*Kneels.*]
Alon. Now all the blessings
Of a glad father compass thee about!
Arise, and say how thou camest here. 210
Mir. O, wonder!
How many goodly creatures are there here!
How beauteous mankind is! O brave new world
That has such people in't!
Pros. 'Tis new to thee. 215

218. **Your eld'st acquaintance cannot be three hours:** i.e., you cannot have known each other quite three hours.

230. **hers:** her father; i.e., I welcome her as a daughter.

235. **heaviness:** sorrow; distressing circumstance.

236. **inly:** inwardly.

Alon. What is this maid with whom thou wast at
    play?
Your eld'st acquaintance cannot be three hours.
Is she the goddess that hath severed us
And brought us thus together? 220
    Fer.   Sir, she is mortal;
But by immortal providence she's mine.
I chose her when I could not ask my father
For his advice, nor thought I had one. She
Is daughter to this famous Duke of Milan, 225
Of whom so often I have heard renown
But never saw before; of whom I have
Received a second life; and second father
This lady makes him to me.
    Alon.   I am hers. 230
But, O, how oddly will it sound that I
Must ask my child forgiveness!
    Pros.   There, sir, stop.
Let us not burden our remembrance with
A heaviness that's gone. 235
    Gon.   I have inly wept,
Or should have spoke ere this. Look down, you gods,
And on this couple drop a blessed crown!
For it is you that have chalked forth the way
Which brought us hither. 240
    Alon.   I say amen, Gonzalo.
    Gon. Was Milan thrust from Milan that his issue
Should become kings of Naples? O, rejoice
Beyond a common joy, and set it down
With gold on lasting pillars: In one voyage 245

253. **still:** ever, as at IV. i. 121.

258. **blasphemy:** blasphemous one (addressed to the boatswain).

259. **swearst grace o'erboard:** drive divine favor overboard with your profanity.

263. **glasses:** revolutions of the hourglass; i.e., hours, as at I. ii. 285.

264. **yare:** ready (for sea); seaworthy.

268. **tricksy:** clever.

Did Claribel her husband find at Tunis,
And Ferdinand her brother found a wife
Where he himself was lost; Prospero his dukedom
In a poor isle; and all of us ourselves
When no man was his own.   250

   Alon. [*To Ferdinand and Miranda*] Give me your
     hands.
Let grief and sorrow still embrace his heart
That doth not wish you joy.

   Gon.   Be it so! Amen!   255

    Enter Ariel, with the Master and Boatswain
       amazedly following.

O, look, sir; look, sir! Here is more of us!
I prophesied, if a gallows were on land,
This fellow could not drown. Now, blasphemy,
That swearst grace o'erboard, not an oath on shore?
Hast thou no mouth by land? What is the news?   260

   Boats. The best news is that we have safely found
Our king and company; the next, our ship,
Which, but three glasses since, we gave out split,
Is tight and yare and bravely rigged as when
We first put out to sea.   265

   Ariel. [*Aside to Prospero*] Sir, all this service
Have I done since I went.

   Pros. [*Aside to Ariel*] My tricksy spirit!

   Alon. These are not natural events; they strengthen
From strange to stranger. Say, how came you hither? 270

   Boats. If I did think, sir, I were well awake,

276. **mo:** more, as at II. i. 141.

280. **On a trice:** in a minute; **so please you:** if you please (a conventionally polite phrase).

282. **Moping:** trancedly; in an unconscious state.

284. **diligence:** diligent one.

287-88. **there is in this business more than nature/Was ever conduct of:** i.e., this business is more than natural.

291. **infest:** disturb; **beating:** harping.

292. **picked leisure:** a specially selected time.

293. **single:** I alone (without an oracle).

294-95. **every/These happened accidents:** all of these occurrences. **Accidents** means simply "events."

296. **think of each thing well:** regard everything in the best light; have faith that all is for the best.

I'ld strive to tell you. We were dead of sleep
And (how we know not) all clapped under hatches,
Where, but even now, with strange and several noises
Of roaring, shrieking, howling, jingling chains,　　　275
And mo diversity of sounds, all horrible,
We were awaked; straightway at liberty;
Where we, in all her trim, freshly beheld
Our royal, good and gallant ship, our master
Cap'ring to eye her. On a trice, so please you,　　　280
Even in a dream, were we divided from them
And were brought moping hither.
　　Ariel. [*Aside to Prospero*]　　　Was't well done?
　　Pros. [*Aside to Ariel*] Bravely, my diligence.
　　　Thou shalt be free.　　　285
　　Alon. This is as strange a maze as e'er men trod,
And there is in this business more than nature
Was ever conduct of. Some oracle
Must rectify our knowledge.
　　Pros.　　　　　　Sir, my liege,　　　290
Do not infest your mind with beating on
The strangeness of this business. At picked leisure,
Which shall be shortly, single I'll resolve you
(Which to you shall seem probable) of every
These happened accidents; till when, be cheerful　　　295
And think of each thing well. [*Aside to Ariel*] Come
　　hither, spirit.
Set Caliban and his companions free.
Untie the spell. [*Exit Ariel.*] How fares my gracious
　　sir?　　　300
There are yet missing of your company
Some few odd lads that you remember not.

303-4. **Every . . . himself:** the reverse of the proverbial "Every man for himself."

305. **Coragio:** courage; **bully-monster:** i.e., monster, my hearty. **Bully** is an adjective of comradely approval.

306. **spies:** eyes.

309. **fine:** finely dressed (as the Duke of Milan).

316. **badges:** the clothing which they appropriated symbolizes dishonesty, just as the **badges** of servants symbolize their loyalty to certain great lords.

317. **true:** meaning both "faithful" and "honest."

321. **demidevil:** Caliban's mother was a witch and his father a demon; hence, he is half-human, half-devil.

*Enter Ariel, driving in Caliban, Stephano, and
Trinculo, in their stol'n apparel.*

Ste. Every man shift for all the rest, and let no
man take care for himself; for all is but fortune.
Coragio, bully-monster, coragio!   305

Trin. If these be true spies which I wear in my
head, here's a goodly sight.

Cal. O Setebos, these be brave spirits indeed!
How fine my master is! I am afraid
He will chastise me.   310

Seb.   Ha, ha!
What things are these, my Lord Antonio?
Will money buy 'em?

Ant.   Very like. One of them
Is a plain fish and no doubt marketable.   315

Pros. Mark but the badges of these men, my lords,
Then say if they be true. This misshapen knave,
His mother was a witch, and one so strong
That could control the moon, make flows and ebbs,
And deal in her command without her power.   320
These three have robbed me, and this demidevil
(For he's a bastard one) had plotted with them
To take my life. Two of these fellows you
Must know and own; this thing of darkness I
Acknowledge mine.   325

Cal.   I shall be pinched to death.

Alon. Is not this Stephano, my drunken butler?

Seb. He is drunk now. Where had he wine?

329. **reeling ripe:** almost reeling from the wine he has drunk.

331. **gilded:** flushed (with drink), with possibly also a reference to the finery they wear.

335. **fly-blowing:** Trinculo refers to the saturation he has had in the foul pond, which will repel even flies.

Alon. And Trinculo is reeling ripe. Where should
   they   330
Find this grand liquor that hath gilded 'em?
How camest thou in this pickle?

Trin. I have been in such a pickle, since I saw you
last, that I fear me will never out of my bones. I shall
not fear fly-blowing.   335

Seb. Why, how now, Stephano?

Ste. O, touch me not! I am not Stephano, but a
   cramp.

Pros. You'ld be king o' the isle, sirrah?

Ste. I should have been a sore one then.   340

Alon. This is as strange a thing as e'er I looked on.

Pros. He is as disproportioned in his manners
As in his shape. Go, sirrah, to my cell;
Take with you your companions. As you look
To have my pardon, trim it handsomely.   345

Cal. Ay, that I will! and I'll be wise hereafter,
And seek for grace. What a thrice-double ass
Was I to take this drunkard for a god
And worship this dull fool!

Pros.   Go to! Away!   350

Alon. Hence, and bestow your luggage where you
   found it.

Seb. Or stole it rather.

        [*Exeunt Caliban, Stephano, and Trinculo.*]

Pros. Sir, I invite your Highness and your train
To my poor cell, where you shall take your rest   355
For this one night; which, part of it, I'll waste
With such discourse as, I not doubt, shall make it
Go quick away—the story of my life,

359. **accidents:** events; see l. 295.

368. **Take the ear:** enchant; hold the listener spellbound.

And the particular accidents gone by
Since I came to this isle; and in the morn   360
I'll bring you to your ship, and so to Naples,
Where I have hope to see the nuptial
Of these our dear-beloved solemnized;
And thence retire me to my Milan, where
Every third thought shall be my grave.   365
    Alon.   I long
To hear the story of your life, which must
Take the ear strangely.
    Pros.   I'll deliver all;
And promise you calm seas, auspicious gales,   370
And sail so expeditious that shall catch
Your royal fleet far off.—My Ariel, chick,
That is thy charge. Then to the elements
Be free, and fare thou well.—Please you draw near.
                        Exeunt omnes.

Epi. The playwright's plea, spoken by Prospero, for an indulgent reception of his play.

<hr>

11. **Gentle breath:** kind words.
13. **want:** lack.

EPILOGUE

Spoken by Prospero.

Now my charms are all o'erthrown,
And what strength I have's mine own,
Which is most faint. Now 'tis true
I must be here confined by you,
Or sent to Naples. Let me not,   5
Since I have my dukedom got
And pardoned the deceiver, dwell
In this bare island by your spell;
But release me from my bands
With the help of your good hands.   10
Gentle breath of yours my sails
Must fill, or else my project fails,
Which was to please. Now I want
Spirits to enforce, art to enchant;
And my ending is despair   15
Unless I be relieved by prayer,
Which pierces so that it assaults
Mercy itself and frees all faults.
As you from crimes would pardoned be,
Let your indulgence set me free.   20

Exit.

KEY TO

Famous Lines and Phrases

Methinks he hath no drowning mark upon him;
his complexion is perfect gallows.   [*Gonzalo*—I. i. 28-30]

In the dark backward and abysm of time.   [*Prospero*—I. ii. 61]

The still-vexed Bermoothes.   [*Ariel*—I. ii. 273]

You taught me language, and my profit on't
Is, I know how to curse.   [*Caliban*—I. ii. 444-45]

Song. Come unto these yellow sands.   [*Ariel*—I. ii. 459-71]

Song. Full fathom five thy father lies.   [*Ariel*—I. ii. 482-90]

There's nothing ill can dwell in such a temple.
If the ill spirit have so fair a house,
Good things will strive to dwell with't. [*Miranda*—I. ii. 558-60]

He receives comfort like cold porridge.   [*Sebastian*—II. i. 11]

What's past is prologue.   [*Antonio*—II. i. 288]

They'll take suggestion as a cat laps milk. [*Antonio*—II. i. 328]

Misery acquaints a man with strange bedfellows.
[*Trinculo*—II. ii. 40-1]

Keep a good tongue in your head.   [*Stephano*—III. ii. 35]

The isle is full of noises,
Sounds, and sweet airs that give delight and hurt not . . .
[*Caliban*—III. ii. 140-48]

Our revels now are ended. These our actors,
As I foretold you, were all spirits and
Are melted into air, into thin air . . .
     We are such stuff
As dreams are made on, and our little life
Is rounded with a sleep.   [*Prospero*—IV. i. 167-77]

Ye elves of hills, brooks, standing lakes, and groves . . .
And deeper than did ever plummet sound
I'll drown my book.   [*Prospero*—V. i. 39-64]

Song. Where the bee sucks, there suck I. [*Ariel*—V. i. 96-102]

How many goodly creatures are there here!
How beauteous mankind is! O brave new world
That has such people in't!   [*Miranda*—V. i. 212-14]